In the Pink

. . . .

Also by Susan McBride

Little Black Dress
The Cougar Club
Too Pretty to Die
Night of the Living Deb
The Lone Star Lonely Hearts Club
The Good Girl's Guide to Murder
Blue Blood

IN THE PINK

....

How I Met the Perfect (Younger) Man,
Survived Breast Cancer,
and Found True Happiness After 40

SUSAN MCBRIDE

wm
WILLIAM MORROW
An Imprint of HarperCollinsPublishers

Excerpt from *The Truth About Love and Lightning* copyright © 2013 by Susan McBride.

EPub Edition OCTOBER 2012 ISBN: 9780062230751
Print Edition ISBN: 9780062230768

10 9 8 7 6 5 4 3 2

To Ed and Emily.
I love you more than words can say!

Introduction

WHEN MY WONDERFUL editor, Lucia Macro, asked if I'd be interested in writing about my experience with breast cancer, I leaped at the chance. Since my diagnosis in December of 2006 at age forty-two, I've openly talked about my "boobal trauma," often speaking to women's groups and at fund-raising events for nonprofits that support research, diagnosis, prevention, and the well-being of survivors. I figure that, the more we know and share, the better off we all are . . . and the more we realize we're not in this alone. My experience made me part of a big Pink Army, and whenever I'm around fellow survivors I feel such a rush of energy and positivity. There is nothing like pressing past what frightens us most to make us appreciate the simple things. We suddenly reevaluate everything we thought was necessary, realize what's important, and rid our time of people and things that drag us down. It's no wonder survivors are so upbeat. We don't take anything for granted, least of all our health. We don't take crap anymore either. That's one side effect I wish I could bottle and sell!

But the tale of "me, my boob, and I" goes beyond my diagnosis. The journey to discovering my true self—my better self—started a few years before that. The big turning point for me came when I hit forty, an age when our society seems to think a woman's shelf life has met its expiration date. So many advertisements tell us that to be viable beyond our thirties we must turn into middle-aged Barbies, Botoxing away our lines (and expressions!) and Spanxing away unsightly bulges. Why the heck we'd want to aspire to fakeness boggles my brain! I say, forty is when we should kick convention in the ass. It's the perfect time to enjoy life full-throttle and accept the skin we're in, wrinkles and all.

In the past seven years since crossing the big 4–0, I've experienced so much more than I had in all the years before: more meaningful friendships, deeper love, greater self-acceptance, and true fulfillment in my career. This "second act" has been eye-opening, transformative, and glorious in so many ways. So I can't help but wish the same for every woman out there. I want to spread the word that getting older can be the most amazing time in our lives. We don't need to relive our youth. We just need to hold on to that childlike sense of wonder, ever-curious about the world around us, eager to laugh, our hearts wide open.

What I hope my story conveys is precisely what I look forward to telling my daughter someday: it is never too late to find happiness. You are never too old to do what you want to do or be who you want to be. Life is a ladder, each rung a step toward our best selves and our greatest accomplishments. Surprises await us the higher we climb, some good and some bad, but each teaching us a bit about ourselves that we needed to learn; showing us a part of the world we'd never seen before; and opening our souls so that every emotion we feel is all the more intense.

Here's to love, whenever we find it; to celebrating success, big and small; and to slogging through the crap so we can come out the other side stronger . . . and remain "in the pink" for the rest of our lives.

Susan McBride
June 14, 2012

Books & Boys . . .

Chapter One

*Please, find a man for my daughter so she
doesn't end up a Crazy Cat Lady.*

TURNING FORTY DIDN'T faze me.

Reaching twenty and leaving my teens behind felt far
more unsettling. Even thirty seemed more pivotal, since
that's the age when we're supposed to get our act together,
be invested, own property, and leave singlehood behind for
suburbia, procreation, and minivans.

Still, I wasn't at all sad at bidding adieu to my thirties.
They'd been a great learning curve, a chance to see some
major goals accomplished; namely, getting published and
beginning my professional writing career after more than a

decade filled with hard work and rejection. Being able to support myself doing something I love was a gift, and I treasured it all the more because it had not come without great sacrifice. In the years I'd spent working to get my foot in the door, I'd endured lots of rejection from the publishing world and plenty of digs from less than true believers inside and outside my family, like the jerk at my grandmother's funeral who strongly suggested I "hang it up." (Somehow, I refrained from punching him in the nose.)

My odd jobs had kept my bills paid, and I had saved enough to buy a condo that I filled with furniture and doodads I'd been collecting in anticipation of finally jumping into the wonderful world of thirty-year mortgages. Finally, at forty, I felt settled, like a bird who'd built a really cool nest, and it didn't bother me that I hadn't met Mr. Right to share it with.

Heck, I hadn't even met Mr. Maybe. But I had good friends and a good life. I was downright content and didn't feel incomplete in any sense. Not until I got a kick in the pants in the form of a less than stellar physical exam. My cholesterol was too high (who knew that Snickers wasn't a vegetable?) and I had palpitations due to anxiety. My maternal grandfather had died after multiple heart attacks, and it unnerved me to think that I could be heading down that path.

My internist at the time suggested I find some way to better deal with stress. "Why don't you start drinking?" she suggested (she was totally serious). Since I'm not fond of alcohol, I went cold turkey on junk food, eating lots of fruits and vegetables and no red meat. I began to work out with a vengeance. Within six weeks, I'd toned up, dropped several sizes, gained strength and stamina, and lowered my total cholesterol from the mid–200s to 187. An added benefit: my heart rate quit accelerating like a Lamborghini on crack whenever I found myself worrying (which was often enough—I'm a natural-born Type A).

Fueled by renewed energy and a surge of confidence, I set up a shoot for a new author photo, meeting with a renowned photographer in St. Louis who initially deemed me "too skinny" and advised I "eat some steak" to prepare for the appointment. (Definitely the first time in my life I'd been called "too skinny" by anyone.) The makeup artist flipped out my "anchorwoman hair" in a very cool, messy style that I ended up adopting postshoot. Not only did I get some great photos out of that session (which I'll be using until I'm ninety-three and on a walker), but I felt reborn, like the new, improved me!

That photo session occurred in July of 2005, four months shy of my forty-first birthday; yet I felt younger than ever, both inside and out. Inspired by the positive changes in my health and body—and the forward trajectory of my writing career, sparked by surprisingly good sales of *Blue Blood* and the release of my second series mystery, *The Good Girl's Guide to Murder*—I had a newfound desire to step out of my comfort zone. I would carve out precious time to try new restaurants, see exhibits at local museums, and expand my social circle as well as my horizons.

That included a conscious decision to be more open about the men I met and not shut anyone down just because he didn't look a particular way or wore funny shoes (my mom likes to remind me of a brilliant guy I dumped in high school because of his fondness for desert boots). To be honest, I'd spent a lot of time in my adult life avoiding the dating scene, preferring to be alone—say, reading a good book—rather than waste my time with some random dude just for the sake of going out. Not being much of a drinker, I was never big on the bar or club scene.

But as forty-one came and went, and I was still single— albeit happily—I figured it wouldn't hurt to change my list of "must-haves" regarding men, which hadn't altered much since high school. I needed to look less at the physical package and more at what was inside. My new and improved ideals basically came down to this:

Does he make me laugh?

Do we have plenty to talk about?

Does he keep me on my toes?

Does he smell good?

Does he eat with utensils?

Does he drive his own car and not live with his mother?

These new criteria certainly opened up a brave, new dating world.

It inspired me to say yes more often than no, and my social life blossomed. Still I didn't seem to meet anyone who floated my boat. Perhaps I was meant to be a modern-day Amelia Earhart, albeit flying without a copilot (minus the disappearing-from-the-face-of-the-earth part).

My boyfriendless state concerned my family far more than it did me, as one of my male cousins approached me privately during the weekend of my brother's wedding and asked, "Are you a lesbian? Because if you are that's okay."

I told him that, while I wasn't a lesbian, I appreciated that he was so open-minded.

"I just can't find the right guy," I confessed, thinking surely I couldn't be the only single woman over forty on the planet who hadn't yet met her Prince Charming.

Call me Pollyanna, but I didn't dwell on my state of singlehood often. My days were filled with writing the books I loved, my weekends were often spent traveling, and my friends and family filled any space between. Yet no matter how I expressed my satisfaction with my life, my mother feared that I was destined to become a Crazy Cat Lady (though I had only two cats!), shuffling around in bathrobe and slippers, cleaning litter boxes in between book deadlines.

I think it made her even more nervous that I wasn't afraid of being alone for the rest of my life. My philosophy: if that was how it worked out, that was how it worked out. It wasn't like I was going to mail-order a groom from Russia or Thailand. I didn't feel like I was missing out, even when I got cards and e-mails from friends with photos of their spouses and children. Not everyone is meant to go the marriage-with-two-point-five-kids route.

Surely I wasn't the only female who didn't obsess over weddings or buy bridal magazines and pore through them, picking out wedding dresses well before finding my mate and falling madly in love.

Perhaps I was just being practical, having read a study

that insisted a woman over forty had a better chance of being killed by a terrorist than she did getting hitched. Or else I was too set in my ways, content with doing things on my own terms, never having to compromise (not a bad thing!).

Yes, there were times when I pondered how lovely it would be to have a committed hand to hold and adoring eyes to gaze at over candlelight, a best friend slash lover who understood me like no one else.

"So you'd get married if you found the right man?" my mom would ask now and then, just to reassure herself.

"I would certainly consider it," I'd say. "So long as I was really in love and we could live in a duplex so I could lock myself inside my half when I needed privacy."

"I'm sure that would be just fine," she'd reply, and pat my hand, a hopeful—or was it delusional?—smile on her face.

I realized quickly enough that Mom's deep-seated need to marry me off was bound tightly to her desire to have a grandchild. Though my younger brother was newly married, he and his bride seemed in no hurry to pop out the rug rats. So I think my mother was putting all my eggs in *her* basket.

What happened next is something straight out of a TV sitcom: my enterprising mom took it upon herself to send an e-mail to *St. Louis Magazine*, at the time searching for a new crop of "top singles" for their November 2005 issue. If I had the e-mail right now, I'd share it; but, unfortunately, I don't. All I know is that she said something akin to "Please, find a man for my daughter so she doesn't end up a Crazy Cat Lady."

The magazine took the bait and sent me a questionnaire as they narrowed down likely candidates. It wasn't but a few months later that I learned I was one of ten women selected (only two of us over forty). They chose ten men as well (one over forty). Reminding myself of my promise to broaden my dating horizons—and the fact that I had a third mystery coming out, *The Lone Star Lonely Hearts Club*, appropriately enough—I figured, "What have I got to lose?" And I jumped in wholeheartedly.

At the September photo shoot with the other nineteen singles, I met a handful who would become friends throughout the process. One of them, Jeremy Nolle, was a software applications engineer. Not only was he smart, but he was very good-looking (I hadn't realized they made computer geeks who appeared to have leaped off the pages of *GQ*!). He was also twentysomething, too young for me. But there were no rules against having younger male friends, right?

The party to debut the 2005 "top singles" issue on November 3, 2005, was held at the Contemporary Art Museum in downtown St. Louis. Somehow, I managed to find Jeremy amidst the three hundred or so people in attendance. I wanted to set him up with my older sister, who happened to be (um, still happens to be!) a serial dater of younger men. I was chatting with Jeremy when several of his coworkers showed up. One was tall and slim with dark hair, a shy smile, and warm brown eyes. "This is Ed," Jeremy said, and we aimlessly babbled over the very loud music.

Though I had no idea at the time, meeting Ed that night would change my life.

Chapter Two

If he knocks you up and leaves you,
I'll help take care of the baby.

TALKING TO ED at the magazine's release party was difficult with so many people around and the DJ playing every eighties rock song he had in his cache. So Ed gave me his card, which I promptly lost. I wasn't even sure I'd ever see him again. He had such a baby face that I wondered about his age. One of the other top singles who knew his family told me he was twenty-five or twenty-six. Despite his cuteness factor, a fifteen-year age difference seemed a lot to digest. The only other time I'd dated a younger guy was back in high school, and our age difference was about one year.

I didn't have to wonder "would I or wouldn't I" for long. That next week Ed e-mailed me through *St. Louis Magazine*, asking me to my first-ever hockey game.

What the heck? I thought, and quickly accepted. It would give me a chance to find out exactly how old he was and to see if we had anything in common. If we couldn't carry on a conversation, it wouldn't matter if he was five years younger or fifteen.

Not only did I take my first ride on the MetroLink that night—and witness more than a few bruising hockey fights—but I learned some vital information: Ed was thirty-one, about to turn thirty-two in a couple of months. Even better, he and I had a lot in common, including our wacky sense of humor. I could tell he was generally a quiet guy, but we managed to find endless things to talk about. Oh yeah, and I realized that hockey arenas are incredibly cold, particularly in November. So much for dressing like a fashionista—I nearly froze my tush off!

I didn't kiss him when he took me home. As attractive as he was, I wasn't sure if what I felt was true chemistry or a meeting of like minds, but I was anxious to see where things went. I had a good feeling about him, along the lines of "Even if this doesn't turn into a great love story, I could hang out with this dude now and then."

In the meantime, like a diligent mystery author, I Googled Ed's name and found several facts he'd been too modest to share. First, Ed held his doctorate in computer science, which I knew would thrill my mother. She'd always hoped I'd find a doctor, and I was pretty sure she wouldn't care if he was a doctor of computers rather than people. I also learned that his father was a well-respected professor at Washington University. And, most fun of all, that Ed was the "parent" to a tiger at the St. Louis Zoo. I figured that meant he liked cats, which was a plus since I had two.

Not long after the hockey game, we had our second date, although technically it wasn't really a date. Instead, Ed attended a bachelor/bachelorette auction at a downtown bar. Lots of local celebrity types were participating along with a handful of the *St. Louis Magazine* top singles. We were "sold" to the highest bidders in the name of charity, and Ed showed up after being out of town for a few days, pocketing a roll of cash, ready to pay whatever was necessary to "buy" me. I know, I know. Sweet, huh? And it was a great relief when he outbid a creepy guy in a green shirt.

His payoff: I arranged a night out for us, which involved dinner at my favorite neighborhood Italian restaurant and a movie. Despite our table in the restaurant's basement (albeit a very nice basement), which led us to joking about being near enough to the laundry room to do the linens, and seeing a movie made from the book of an author friend that wasn't exactly date-appropriate, we had a great time. As at the hockey game, we talked pretty much nonstop (except during the movie). When he took me home, I let him kiss me, and it was a very good kiss. I also blurted out as he was departing, "You're a really nice guy, Ed Spitznagel."

He gave me a funny look, and the next day, I got an e-mail that read: "If you ever call me 'nice' again, I'll have to spank you."

Ha! I thought that was hilarious! And I let him know that being nice was a good thing in my book. I wasn't one of those women who lusted after bad boys. Boy Scouts were more my style. Finding a guy who said what he meant and kept his promises felt a little like winning the lottery. That chemistry I had wondered about earlier? Oh, it was there in spades. Being with Ed made me giddy in a way I hadn't been since college.

To top it off, he composed the most wonderful e-mails, warm and clever and always grammatical. His spelling was impeccable, which I found refreshing after receiving too many notes from guys who clearly didn't use dictionaries or comprehend how punctuation worked. So when I happily told my mom, "Ed even knows how to use a semicolon!" she was ready to book the church.

Since Ed frequently got carded when we ate out—like, nine out of ten times—occasionally the question about our age difference would rear its ugly head. Did it look to the world like I was his mother? That was my main concern! Otherwise, I didn't care, and I hoped it didn't bother him either. Still, he did look awfully young for his age, and no matter how fabulous I felt at forty-one, I clearly was the older one of the pair.

One truly uncomfortable moment came while we were out at an Italian restaurant chain, and our waitress said I reminded her of someone she knew, and was I, perhaps, the mother of her eighteen-year-old friend Sasha. "No," I told her, although I realized I could have been. "I don't have kids." What I really wanted to say was *Aw, too bad, sweetie. There went your tip.*

"It doesn't matter," Ed would assure me, and I would agree. But that didn't mean we didn't get ribbed about it fairly often.

My real cougar sister was the first to start calling me a cougar, a term I was only familiar with because of tabloid magazine fodder relating to Hollywood actresses like Cher and Demi Moore. "I'm *not* a cougar," I insisted. "I'm just an accidental cougar!" Ed had done the chasing, not me. I'd never been fond of animal prints, had never crashed a frat party to pick up a college boy, and I had no desire to laser or Botox my face (or any other part of my anatomy).

Although being called a cougar did have its merits. My editor would soon ask me to consider writing a novel about forty-something women who date younger men ("so long as it isn't cheesy," I insisted, and ended up penning *The Cougar Club*, released in late January of 2010).

As I'd later learn, Ed's mother was concerned about my cougar-dom, too. I couldn't hide my age from her as it was there in black and white in the November 2005 issue of *St. Louis Magazine*. But I hoped that when she had the chance to meet me, she'd see I was hardly a modern-day Mrs. Robinson.

Despite telling myself to take it slow, Ed and I began spending lots of time together. He showed up at my book signings, including one at Big Sleep Books in early December of 2005, where we flirted and held hands, causing the owner of the store, Helen Simpson, to whisper in my mother's ear, "They'd make such beautiful babies!" I think Helen was as anxious as my mom that I find a good man.

After more dates, book events, and lots of e-mails, I invited Ed to my folks' house for Christmas Eve dinner. By then, I knew something special was going on. I could hardly write my next mystery for thinking about him. And when I wasn't thinking about him, he was over at my place or we were out doing something fun, like freezing our butts off at the St. Louis Zoo to see the Wild Lights display that ran throughout the winter holidays.

When he came to pick me up for the meet-the-folks dinner, he was wearing a neon-green and black striped shirt. In the past I'd been rather picky about how my dates dressed. Which is how my mom knew it was true love even before I did. "His shirt was awful, and you didn't care," she said to me the next day. I think my mom and dad fell a little in love with Ed that night as well. They could see he was good for me and sharp enough that I'd never get bored. And it inspired visions of grandkids dancing in my mother's head. "If he knocks you up and leaves you," she said, "I'll help take care of the baby."

I'm not kidding.

Sometime after the New Year, I had the privilege of meeting Ed's family to celebrate his thirty-second birthday. I remember sitting across from his dad in a booth at the Cheesecake Factory, and I liked Big Ed right away as he laughed at my jokes.

Of course, I worried what Ed's mom was thinking, though we did a girls' bathroom break and I got to chitchat with her for a bit. She seemed so down-to-earth and sweet, and I just hoped I was making a good impression. I really wanted her to see how much I cared for her son and not assume I was some older chick taking advantage of him. (Later, she would confess that Ed had told her he was bringing his "better half" to his birthday dinner, to which she'd replied, "Do you know what you're saying?")

In early February, I gave Ed a key to condo-sit when I had to leave for a mystery conference in Birmingham. Even after I returned, he never really left, mostly living at my place with me and my cats, Max and Munch. Within a few more weeks, I knew without a doubt that this was the real deal. We had both said, "I love you" already, and I believed it to be true. I even changed my mind about needing a duplex. I didn't want to separate myself from him. I loved being with Ed, and he gave me the space I needed without having to lock him out. He allowed me to be me, and I let him be him, although I did slowly but surely encourage him to get rid of that neon-green and black striped shirt (among a few other things).

Being an honest-to-a-fault woman who didn't want to play fast and loose with her heart, I gave him an ultimatum . . . on Valentine's Day. (Yep, you read that right.) I needed to hear that I was "the one" for him and that he was in this relationship for the long haul. I couldn't keep falling deeper in love with him if he didn't feel the same. He left for work that morning with me on the verge of tears (yeah, Happy V-Day, suckers!). I called my mom once he'd headed out and told her what I'd done.

"That's it. He's not coming back," she said point-blank.

Thanks for the vote of confidence, Ma.

But she was wrong. After work that night, he came home to the condo with an armful of roses. And more importantly, he said, "You're the one."

"You have no doubts?"

"None." He shook his head.

And I could finally breathe.

Every day we were together was the best day of my life. There were times in the past when I'd imagined I was in love; but until Ed, I'd never experienced unconditional love, the kind that deepens and makes you appreciate all the things in your partner that you are not. I couldn't imagine my world without him in it.

By June of 2006, we were house hunting. We bought a place—actually, the first house we saw, though we did look at others—and moved in together that July. I got caught up in putting our new digs together, supervising painters and electricians, all the while working on a deadline for two books, my fifth series mystery for Avon called *Too Pretty to Die* and a nonmystery young adult series book for Random House called *The Debs*. Every day felt exhausting, and I neglected myself in the process, including doing my monthly breast self-exams because "I didn't have time."

I know. Horrible excuse.

So when I went to my doctor for an annual physical, and she told me I had a cyst in my left breast, I wasn't surprised. I'd had cysts before. Only this one wasn't like any of the others. It ended up being something else entirely, something that would yank the rug right out from under my feet and put my relationship with Ed to the test.

"You have no doubts?"

"None." He shook his head.

And I could finally breathe.

Every day we were together was the best day of my life. There were times in the past when I'd imagined I was in love, but until Ed, I'd never experienced unconditional love, the kind that deepens and makes you appreciate all the things in your partner that you are not. I couldn't imagine my world without him in it.

By June of 2006, we were house hunting. We bought a place—actually, the first house we saw, though we did look at others—and moved in together that July. I got caught up in putting our new digs together, supervising painters and electricians, all the while working on a deadline for two books, my fifth series mystery for Avon called *Too Pretty to Die* and a nonmystery young adult series book for Random House called *The Debs*. Every day felt exhausting, and I neglected myself in the process, including doing my monthly breast self-exams because "I didn't have time."

I know. Horrible excuse.

So when I went to my doctor for an annual physical, and she told me I had a cyst in my left breast, I wasn't surprised. I'd had cysts before. Only this one wasn't like any of the others. It ended up being something else entirely, something that would yank the rug right out from under my life and put my relationship with Ed to the test.

Boobs . . .

Chapter Three

It's (not) just a cyst.

MY GRANDMOTHER HAD breast cancer when I was in grade school. I distinctly remember my mom crying and telling us she had to go to St. Louis to take care of *her* mom. But, of course, I didn't understand what was going on, just that my grandma was sick.

When I saw Grandma that summer, she talked about having a mastectomy and sticking a prosthesis in her bra; but I had no idea what any of that meant. I was just happy she seemed well again, clearly having recovered from whatever had ailed her. She was as feisty (and bossy) as ever. I didn't notice any difference.

Boobs were not something much discussed in those days, except when some of the wild boys in fifth grade used to chase us girls around, yelling, "Titty twisters!" and grabbing at our chests, even if there wasn't anything to grab.

My family was rather conservative. We didn't talk about emotions, much less about body parts, which didn't seem important until I was in junior high and sprouted breasts. My sister and I were on a gymnastics team then, clad in leotards for hours after school each day. Molly was slow to develop. I was not. Even though my budding boobs barely required a training bra, I was still the "biggest" on the team for a long while (until we had three eighteen-year-olds join up). I was very self-conscious and often wore big T-shirts over my leotards at practice. For years after, I felt like I was overly endowed, until other girls began growing breasts far larger.

I don't recall anyone ever expressing concern that I was at a higher risk for breast cancer than the average female. Indeed, when I was a young adult and the issue came up with my gynecologist, I was told that my maternal grandmother's diagnosis did not put me in any extra danger. My mother and her sister, my aunt Mary, were fine. No one on my father's side had ever had breast cancer that I was aware of.

However, I did have a baseline mammogram at thirty-five and began to have them yearly at age forty, mostly because I had dense breast tissue and tended toward cysts. Every now and then I'd call my doctor, concerned about feeling a lump. She would examine me, assure me that what I felt was benign, and it would eventually go away. After years of this pattern,

I may have even gotten a little blasé about feeling the occasional bump on self-exam.

In fact, in August of 2006 when I went in for a routine exam and my doctor pointed out that I had another "cyst," I was truly unconcerned. "Here," she told me, "feel this. Did you know it was there?"

"No," I told her, because I hadn't noticed. I was so busy with movers and painters and electricians—and the inevitable book deadline—that I hadn't taken the time to do a recent self-exam.

Because of my past history, she was convinced it was nothing to worry about, and I was doubly reassured by the fact that my annual mammogram was forthcoming on September 11. (*Cue ominous music!* Definitely a date I will forever after avoid when scheduling mammograms!).

When I went in for the test, I told the technician about the lump. She seemed perplexed that my doctor had ordered a screening mammogram and not a diagnostic scan. "You can call her," I said, "and get the order changed if you're concerned."

Honestly, I just wanted to do the test and get out of there.

The tech did not phone my doctor and the order was not changed, so I had the screening mammogram without any kind of spot check. A week or so after, I got the all-clear letter telling me, "You're fine. See you next year."

I breathed a sigh of relief; but I couldn't completely let it go. Something didn't feel right. Every time I showered, I rubbed the area over the "cyst." It did not seem to be going away and felt awfully hard besides, like a small marble.

"Feel this," I would say to Ed on occasion, and he'd get the funniest look on his face. "Does it seem bigger?" I'd badger, and he'd reply, "I don't know."

Clearly, he was terrified of saying the wrong thing. Men, I decided, do not make good boobometers. They're not wired to say, "Yes, this lump feels weird," any more than they're apt to tell us, "Yes, you do look fat."

So I pretended everything was okay and tried to put the lump out of my mind. My life was so busy that I convinced myself "the mammogram was negative, the doctor thinks you're fine," and I put any fear out of my head, at least for a while.

On December 11, three months after my mammogram, I was at brunch to celebrate my sister's birthday when I felt twinges of pain in my left breast, right in the area of the "cyst." I honestly believe that my body was trying to tell me something and, this time, I listened.

I called my doctor's office the next day, a Monday, and I requested an ultrasound. She agreed to set it up, although she wanted me to come see her again first for an exam. When I saw her and she palpated the area, she again assured me, "It's a cyst. It's just a cyst."

My mother accompanied me to the ultrasound, sitting in the waiting room while I underwent the scan. I tried to keep things light, talking and joking as the ultrasound tech touched the paddle to my left breast after prepping me with gooey gel. I couldn't help but watch the monitor along with her, and I saw the grainy jellybean-shaped blob as soon as she did. Though she maintained a calm demeanor, I sensed a change in her expression—or maybe I was projecting my alarm onto her, I'm not sure which.

"What is it?" I asked, feeling a rising sense of panic.

"It's probably nothing," she said. "But let me get the chief radiologist to take a look." She made sure I was covered and comfortable while I waited for the doctor to appear.

I had a feeling that the lump was something bad even before the radiologist came in, introduced himself, and checked out the area for himself. "We need to do a biopsy," he told me, and I nodded, fighting the urge to bawl. One thing was for sure: I wanted that biopsy done as soon as possible. The ultrasound technician was very kind, relating in a calm voice the high probability that this abnormality was benign.

But as soon as I dressed and found my way back to the front desk—and saw my mom in the waiting room—I burst into tears. "It's bad, I know it," I said, struggling to hold myself together long enough to set up my appointment for a biopsy later that week.

I went home wondering what would happen if I was in that small percentage of women whose results were not benign. How would Ed take it? What would it do to our lives? What about the books I had to write? So many questions raced through my mind that I felt sick to my stomach.

Ed and I were always upfront with each other, so I didn't hide anything from him. I told him what was going on and how scared I was. He's a good listener and a pro at keeping his cool. "It's going to be okay," he said, and squeezed my hand. But I'm not sure any amount of coddling could have made me relax.

The core biopsy itself was a blur. I went back to the same ultrasound room where I'd been the week before. I recall getting numbed so the radiologist could insert needles and withdraw bits of the lesion for pathology. I may have babbled endlessly during the procedure (my typical MO), or I may have said nothing at all. I think I blocked out much of what transpired that day because I was so afraid; and so convinced of rotten news well before my doctor phoned with the results of the biopsy report.

Chapter Four

Am I going to die?

THE CORE BIOPSY results returned just days before Christmas in 2006.

When the phone rang, I answered in our bedroom and heard my doctor's voice. I couldn't sit down. I could hardly stand still. When she said, "You have cancer," the world stopped spinning for an instant. It took a minute to catch my breath. Then I asked the first thing that crossed my mind: "Am I going to die?"

I was only forty-two. I had been with Ed for a year. We had picked out an antique engagement ring and he intended to officially propose over the holidays. I had two book deadlines looming; in fact, I was in the midst of writing *Too Pretty to Die*, the fifth and last of my mystery series. All I could think about was my future, and suddenly I questioned whether I'd have much of a future at all.

"No, you're not going to die," my doctor said quite firmly. "You have something called pure mucinous carcinoma. The prognosis is excellent. But you need to call a breast surgeon and schedule an appointment to discuss surgery and treatment."

Oh boy.

I hated needles, couldn't imagine being cut into, and I wondered if I'd have to do chemotherapy, putting poison in my body to kill the bad with the good.

I was scared out of my mind.

She gave me names, and as soon as I hung up with her, I tearfully phoned the surgical practice. It was close to dinnertime on a Thursday and Christmas was that Monday. I was frantic when I was told the first available appointment I could get with the surgeon to whom my doctor had referred me was weeks and weeks away. I ended up asking, "Is there another surgeon there who could see me before the holiday weekend?"

"Dr. O is available," I was told, and I immediately scheduled an appointment for the next day.

I'm not patient. I'm horrible at waiting. I didn't need more time to ponder what had to be done. I wanted this thing out of my breast ASAP. I felt like an alien had invaded my body, and I envisioned it growing, taking over my organs, and making me weaker and weaker. That was the worst thing about the diagnosis: all of a sudden being told I was ill when I didn't feel ill at all. I felt great, as a matter of fact, the opposite of sick. I couldn't understand how something so small could wreak such havoc. But that's what cancer does: it's subversive and stealthy, sneaking up like a thief in the night, hiding in the shadows, hoping no one will see.

Ed wasn't yet home from work, and I didn't want to call and tell him something so serious over the phone. So I called my mom and burst into tears. "I'll be right over," she said, and appeared on my doorstep within minutes. When I let her in, she gave me a bear hug, crying as I cried, telling me, "If I could take the cancer from you and give it to myself, I would do it in a heartbeat."

I wished someone would take the cancer from me, too, but I didn't want to give it to her. I just wanted it gone.

She stayed with me until Ed arrived home. I heard his car in the driveway and then the garage door opening and I braced myself, leaving my mom in the living room and walking into the kitchen to greet him, hoping I could stay composed. When he came in, and I saw his sweet face, it broke my heart to tell him, "The lump—it's cancerous."

He looked at me with tears in his eyes, and he held me as tightly as he could.

When we drew apart and went into the living room, my mother stared at him and said, "So, are you going to run?"

Did I mention my mother is blunt?

Ed didn't even flinch. "I'm not going anywhere," he told her, exactly what I knew he'd say. And I believed him.

I had several friends who'd gone through a breast cancer

diagnosis before me, and I reached out to them, knowing they'd commiserate. I told my other friends as well, laying out my fears about what was to come. The flood of understanding notes and phone calls buoyed my spirits. There were women I knew from the publishing world who confessed that they were survivors, too. They had kept their diagnoses private so this was the first time I'd heard their stories. As scared as I was, I felt surrounded by support and affection and empathy, although there were several exceptions.

A close friend was noticeably quiet. When I didn't hear from her . . . and didn't hear from her . . . I finally did the reaching out, asking if she was okay. Did she imagine that what I had was catching (that was my gut reaction)? I had to remind myself that everyone responds to bad news differently. Just because she wasn't leaping to throw her arms around me didn't mean she was a terrible person. I'm not sure which was more unsettling: dealing with silence or comments that seemed downright insensitive. The one e-mail I'll never forget said this: "I hope you don't die."

Gee, thanks. Me too.

Though I never found out why the one friend was so silent initially, she did support me throughout, and we're friends to this day. I can't say the same for the one who sent me the "hope you don't die" message. We drifted apart, although there were never any bad feelings.

My goal was to focus on the positive messages, on the hands extended for me to hold, and the shoulders given to lean on. I couldn't let negativity take root in my mind. I had a battle to fight.

When I saw the breast surgeon just before Christmas, I tearfully listened as she explained all my options. From the get-go, I was hoping for breast-conserving lumpectomy with node biopsy, and she seemed confident that would give us good results. So that was what I chose. Surgery was scheduled for December 28, the soonest Dr. O could fit me in. I had all the necessary scans and blood tests in the days beforehand. Every night before I fell asleep, I closed my eyes and focused on being cancer-free. I couldn't wait until the "alien" was gone from beneath my skin.

The rest of my treatment would be determined by the pathology results from the surgery. Only after that report came in would I meet with the radiation oncologist and the oncologist to determine what further course was needed. My cancer was deemed Stage 2a because of the size of the tumor (about three centimeters), not because of anything else seen on the biopsy pathology, so I was hoping like hell to avoid chemotherapy.

I was in love with a younger man who had proposed to me on Christmas Eve. In front of our tree with the bright lights twinkling, he had gotten down on bended knee and asked, "Susan McBride, will you marry me?" I happily said, "Yes" through my tears, and I didn't let Ed go all night. I had no doubt in my mind that this was the man I wanted to be with for life. So while I would do whatever it took to heal, I dreaded the thought of chemo pushing me into early menopause. I wanted to hold on to the chance—no matter how slim—that we could have a baby down the road. Even if it was a pipe dream, it was my dream, and I clung to it.

Though we have pictures from that Christmas of 2006 where Ed and I are smiling, it was a tough one to get through. The best part was sharing the good news that we were engaged and showing our families my quaint antique ring, a brilliant reminder that sometimes the best of times and worst of times can happen at once.

Three days later, I would head to the outpatient facility for surgery, the first step on the rocky path to getting my life back as I knew it.

Chapter Five

You may bleed blue, but I pee blue.

IT WAS NO wonder they instructed me to arrive at the outpatient check-in early. There were five million things to do before they prepped me for surgery, including lots of paperwork. Once that was done, I was sent to have a guide wire inserted into my breast so Dr. O could see the direct route to my tumor. The guide wire insertion wasn't even the worst part of that lovely episode. It was having a mammogram afterward with the wire in place. Getting squashed like a pancake is uncomfortable enough without having hardware hanging out of your boob. (A week after that I got a letter from the facility telling me to contact my doctor immediately as I had an abnormal mammogram. *Oh, really? I wonder why? Duh!*)

Ed was allowed to hang out with me once I was dressed in my gown, hair in a skullcap, and leads connecting me to the monitor that showed my heart rate and blood pressure. I'd already talked to the anesthesiologist and answered a lot of questions, mostly about allergies and stuff. Safely tucked onto the gurney that would take me into surgery, I got my own little curtained space to await Dr. O's appearance. I heard a woman crying in the slot next door, telling her husband, "I don't want to have a re-excision! I just want to go home!" At the time, I didn't know what that meant, but I felt awful for her just the same.

When Ed was told to leave, I spoke to the nurse on hand, remarking that having to undergo nonelective surgery had convinced me that I never wanted to have a facelift or tummy tuck or anything else for that matter.

"Why would you put yourself through this if you didn't have to?" I asked.

"Oh, I want to have my breasts done someday," she told me. "When you work here, having surgery doesn't seem like such a big deal."

It's all in the perspective, I guess.

I realized when Dr. O arrived because of the sound of her footsteps. She's a girlie-girl, for sure, always wearing the most fashionable shoes. Once I heard those heels tip-tapping on the floor, I braced myself. She came over to say, "Hi," and told me about the radioactive dye they were injecting into my body so they could stain the sentinel lymph nodes that were my immune system's first line of defense. I'm sure I said something stupid, like, "Will it make me glow in the dark?"

But the dye didn't make me glow. What it did was cause me to pee blue, about the same color blue as one of those toilet bowl cleaners. That season, the St. Louis Blues hockey team had a motto: "We Bleed Blue." I wished I could have told them that I could top that.

I remember babbling to the surgical team after they'd wheeled me into the operating room. But once the anesthesia was administered, I was out like a light. When I woke up after the surgery, I felt very, very cold. Then I passed out again, only to awaken in recovery. I fought like hell to open my eyes and sit up. I just wanted to go home. It was a while before I could summon a nurse, get some Teddy Grahams and juice, and find my clothes. My chest was so tightly wrapped in a bear-hug bandage that I couldn't feel much of anything except pressure.

Soon enough, they wheeled me into a little room to wait for Ed and my mom. The way Ed's face lit up when he saw me was priceless. My mother would later tell me that he might as well have been holding his breath the entire time I was in the operating room; he was so anxious to see that I'd come out of surgery and could still smile and crack jokes.

The ride home was uneventful except for the sight of two dogs humping in someone's unfenced backyard while we waited at a stoplight. It at least made the three of us laugh, which was something that would become all too important in the weeks and months ahead.

Other than the blue pee and grasping the fact that I needed pain pills to get through the first few days postsurgery—not easy for a girl who doesn't like taking aspirin—my most vivid memory is of removing the bear-hug bandage. My mother was over at the house at the time, but I went into the bathroom alone to unwrap it. I'm not sure why I wanted to be by myself when I first glimpsed my incisions and bruises, but I did. I was standing in front of the mirror as I slowly began unraveling the bandage, layer after layer, like I was peeling an onion. When I got to the end and finally released my breasts and ribs from its grip, I came very close to passing out. I sank down onto the toilet lid and sat for a few minutes until I could take in a few deep breaths. I'd been breathing so shallowly with it on for the previous twenty-four hours that I was out of practice. I must've made some noise, as my mom barged in to see what was going on. She helped me stand and kept an arm around my waist as I looked in the mirror to see my wounds.

My left boob was a virtual rainbow of bruises, the skin all shades of yellow, purple, green, and blue. I had two red incision lines on the left side, one at the site of my lymph node dissection and another longer one at my tumor site. I decided then and there to call that breast Frankenboob. I figured it needed a nickname and that seemed to fit. Despite my attempt at levity, it was a hard thing to digest, no matter that I kept telling myself that I'd kept my breast, that dents and dings and scars made no difference. I was the same person, and staying alive was the name of the game. But it would be a long while before I fully accepted the changes and could gaze at my chest in the mirror without my throat catching.

Something else that came as a surprise: no one had warned me that having sentinel nodes removed from my armpit would cause my arm to feel like it was bound to my side by a string. "They didn't show you how to do wall-walking with your hand?" a friend of mine who'd gone through a lumpectomy asked, seemingly stunned that this vital piece of information hadn't been shared. So she described what to do, and I started trying every day to inch my left hand farther and farther up the wall. I was slowly resuming normal activities around the house as well, emptying the dishwasher and tossing clothes in the washing machine. I figured those were very practical exercises to improve my range of motion.

Though I'd made it past the initial surgery, I wasn't yet in the clear. The two weeks as I waited for my pathology results were the longest of my life. I was hoping for several things: first and foremost, that the surgical path showed pure mucinous carcinoma as the biopsy had. If the mucinous cancer was mixed with any other kind, it would be far trickier to treat. And secondly, I wanted reassurance that Dr. O had gotten all the bad cells out (aka clear margins). I kept thinking of the woman who'd been crying about undergoing a re-excision, and I wondered if that would be me as well. As I'd come to learn, getting re-excised meant going back to the operating room so Dr. O could remove even more tissue to ensure she had not left a single cancer cell behind.

Every night, I prayed for clear margins. I did not want to go back for more surgery. To do so would have felt like taking a step back instead of moving forward.

While I waited, I did the best I could to distract myself.

When Ed went to work each morning, my mom came by and would turn on *Ellen*, knowing that would make me laugh. I had books to write, too, with about one hundred pages of *Too Pretty to Die* still to finish for Avon and *The Debs* to start for Delacorte. It was strange, having to remind myself to be funny as I chipped away at a humorous mystery when I was going through a rough patch that was so incredibly serious. But escaping into my fiction was so cathartic. In my books, I could control the characters and what happened to them, strangely reassuring when I felt completely out of control in my real life.

Beyond the writing, I also had *Night of the Living Deb* releasing in February of 2007, and I had events lined up, starting in a matter of weeks. I didn't know what I'd be able to do or not do, so I pushed those worries away for a while. My motto fast became "One day at a time," because that's about as far ahead as I could look.

When I finally got a call about my pathology results, I knew something wasn't good. It was Dr. O phoning, not her nurse. I took that to mean, *I've got bad news*, and I was right. One margin wasn't clear. There were still cancerous cells in my left breast. I had to go back in for more surgery, scheduled for January 10, 2007: yep, the dreaded re-excision.

I told myself, *It could be worse*. I wasn't going in for a mastectomy. I was just having more tissue removed. I thought of the women I knew—and so many other women out there—who'd had to undergo much more radical surgery than I. In the grand scheme of things, I was getting off pretty lightly.

Throughout my treatment, I kept reminding myself of that fact.

My mom came over the night before my second surgery, and I sat between her and Ed on the bed, each of them holding my hand and being very silly. Despite all the ways I reassured myself, I was still fearful at having to be cut into again when my incisions had had two weeks to start healing. But, somehow, Mom and Ed made me laugh through my tears. They were getting awfully good at breaking up my pity parties.

Damn them.

The morning of my second surgery didn't start out so well. Someone had told us the wrong time to show up, and the woman at check-in had to rush me along the minute I appeared. Though I guess that was better than having to wait. When I was fast-tracked through prep and on the cart, ready to be wheeled into the operating room, Dr. O stopped by, and I asked her point-blank, "How do you know where the bad cells are when you go back in? How do you find the ones left on just one margin of the tumor site? What if you take out the wrong stuff?"

She gave me an odd look. "Susan, do I ask you how you write your books?"

"Good point," I said, and then I was off to surgery again.

Luckily, the path results this time showed all margins were clear and there was no sign of any bad cells having traveled to my lymph nodes. I felt almost as though I could breathe again.

The only thing that kept me from resting easily was knowing I had forthcoming appointments with the oncologist and the radiation oncologist. I realized my treatment was hardly over yet. I only hoped it would be of the less-is-more variety. But the way everyone kept reminding me, "We have to do everything we can to make sure this doesn't come back as you're only forty-two," I worried that my treatment might tend toward overkill.

I worried, too, about Ed's and my relationship. He was my rock and had never let me down, not even for a moment; but I hated that my diagnosis seemed to have taken over everything. I kept saying, "We will get our lives back someday," and I tried to keep his world from turning as upside-down as mine. I insisted he attend Blues games, play with his recreational league hockey team, and attend his work functions. Even if I couldn't be by his side, I didn't want him missing out.

We tried to create quiet times to be together as well, when we didn't talk about my boob, when we could just feel (even for a few minutes) like a couple in love again. And we joked about saying our vows when we got married. Heck, we were already going through the "for worse" part so we figured we were due for a lot of "for better."

I'd like to believe I would have made it through my diagnosis without him. But I can't imagine what it would have been like. Having Ed beside me every step of the way kept me going. I wanted to be well again, not only for myself, but for us. Meeting Ed when I did and falling in love with him was the best thing that ever happened to me. As corny as this may sound, I knew in my heart I was meant to be with him, that we are the truest of soul mates, our age difference be damned.

When I think of all the dominoes that had to fall into place so that I would run into him at that magazine party, I'm amazed that it happened at all. Which reaffirmed my faith in miracles and the idea that we are often guided by something or someone greater than us—God, fate, the universe, Buddha, whatever one chooses to call it—that leads us to exactly where we need to be.

Or, as Ed and I like to joke, our grandmothers got together in Heaven to play some bridge, and one said to the other, "I have this granddaughter who happens to be way too independent for her own good." Only to have the other respond, "Well, I have a grandson who's single with a doctorate and a new job. Should we throw them together?"

If anything, Ed's and my relationship was strengthened because of my cancer. And with more treatment still forthcoming, I needed all the strength I could get.

Chapter Six

It's my body, isn't it?

•

I DID NOT hit it off with the oncologist.

From the get-go, she pushed the idea of chemo, even though I wasn't entirely certain I needed it. To convince me, she pressed hard for a $3,000 genome test to compare my tumor with other tumors and assess the likelihood of my cancer recurring. My insurance company would not pay for the test, and I didn't want it anyway. I'd already boned up on pure mucinous carcinoma, I understood the implications of my pathology results, and I did not want to harm my body more than I had to in order to survive this ordeal.

But the oncologist did not relent, and the constant arm-twisting finally did me in. I was physically and emotionally exhausted, and I wanted to save my fight for my treatment. So I caved on the genome test, after both the testing company and the oncologist's office swore they would take care of the bill. (Oh Lord, that became a fight in itself, as did other bills my insurance didn't cover that began filling my mailbox while I was still in treatment and ended up costing $12,000 out of pocket and a lot of frustration and tears—so don't ask me what I think of how our health-care system operates, as I'll tell you it's a freaking mess.)

The genome test score was low enough that I was on the borderline between "skip the chemo" and the gray area suggesting "it's up to you and your doctor" as far as whether I'd benefit from anything but surgery and radiation.

Ever persistent, the oncologist kept shaking her pro-chemo pom-poms (*"Two, four, six, eight, who do we appreciate? Go, chemo!"*). I had to remind myself that that was her job. Clearly she believed in the stuff, or she'd be in another field. But that didn't mean I had to go along with her.

I remember thinking—and saying—"It's my body, isn't it?" Didn't I get to decide my own path?

Just to cover all my bases, I discussed the situation with my other physicians, including my long-time physician who'd found the lump; my breast surgeon, Dr. O; and Dr. G, the radiation oncologist who would be in charge of my radiation therapy. All of them agreed with me that chemotherapy wasn't necessary for my recovery. When I said, "Thanks, but no," to the oncologist, she was not a happy camper. Ultimately, she and I never gelled, and I was relieved when I was able to cease making appointments with her. Seeing her virtually guaranteed a rise in my blood pressure.

My meeting with Dr. G and the radiation oncology department was another story entirely. I loved everyone in that department the moment I met them. Dr. G was wonderful: open and warm and gung-ho about healthy eating and a healthy lifestyle. The radiation techs were quirky and funny. I couldn't be around them without finding myself in a better mood. Before my sessions could begin, I had to do a CAT scan so they knew exactly where all my organs were situated. Dr. G would map out where precisely the radiation would go, with the goal of avoiding as much lung and heart tissue as she could.

Once the plan was in place, I showed up specifically so they could set up the machine that would shoot the beams into my breast area. That was when they took a laundry marker and drew points around my chest so that the machine and I would line up. I was told to be careful about the markings—something they used to create with tattoos—and that, if I exercised, to dust cornstarch on the dots so they wouldn't erode. At any rate, I was not supposed to touch them up. (Although I must confess that I did repair work now and then, if I got on the treadmill to walk, sweated a bit, and forgot the cornstarch. Oops.)

Dr. G wrote me a prescription for something called Biafine, a cream used on burn patients. I often say the Biafine saved my skin, because it did. I'm so fair and prone to burning, I was afraid I wouldn't make it through thirty-four radiation sessions without bubbling and peeling, which would have delayed continuous treatment. But I started rubbing on the Biafine even before my rad therapy started, and I would highly recommend patients ask their doctors about it (so far as I'm concerned, it puts aloe, vitamin E cream, etc., to shame). After that, we were set, and I began showing up every weekday to get zapped.

My mom and Ed's mom made a pact that one of them would drive me to each of my thirty-four sessions so I would never have to go alone. I will be forever grateful to them both for such a generous act. I scheduled my therapy so it was in the morning. I figured I'd get it done with early and then be able to rest and write the remainder of the day.

A wonderful mystery author and breast cancer survivor gave me some advice for when I was lying on the machine, listening to the noises as it fried my cells. She told me to repeat something like "Kill the bad stuff," over and over until the zapping ceased.

What amazed me most was how mere seconds of being pelted with radiation could have such an impact on my body. Though, unlike chemo, you don't lose your hair with radiation to treat breast cancer—nor do you get a metallic taste in your mouth—you do get very "sunburned" and tired. I'd been warned that I'd need naps every day; but I didn't really feel any soggier than I had postsurgery. Besides, I had to finish up *Too Pretty to Die* and start *The Debs*, and I had that new mystery coming out. If my body needed rest, I rested. If I had the energy, I worked. Being productive was about as close to feeling normal as I would get for a while.

There were also odd sensations that accompanied the rad

therapy. One night, I awakened in the dark, howling with stabbing pains in my chest. It felt like I was having a heart attack. Ed comforted me and talked me down so I didn't dial 911. When I went for my next day's session, I asked the techs, "Was that normal? Or is something wrong?"

I never really got a solid answer to my question, not from the medical staff. I did find out from a friend and fellow survivor that she'd had similar pains, sometimes when out running errands. "Wait'll you get one of those when you're standing in line at the grocery store," she told me.

Oh boy.

On weekends in February and March after *Night of the Living Deb* came out, I kept my schedule of local book signings, appearing at various independent and chain bookstores wearing my best comfort clothes: jeans, a camisole, and a similarly colored zip-up sweatshirt. The Soft Surroundings camisoles were a lifesaver. My chest was way too sore to wear a bra for a long, long while. Those who came out to see me were so supportive. One of my rad techs from Dr. G's office even showed up at Main Street Books wearing a "Save the Ta-Tas" T-shirt, something Ed will never forget!

I did several radio shows during my radiation therapy, too, one for the local NPR station, where I was asked by a caller if I was angry at my doctor who initially told me my lump was a cyst. "No," I replied, and I meant it. "I'm grateful that she found it at all when I wasn't looking."

And who's to say that there wasn't a cyst? When Dr. O removed my tumor, she noticed a "benign growth" attached, which has always left me wondering if that was really what we felt, not the tumor itself.

I did end up canceling the out-of-town appearances during radiation treatment. Initially, I thought I could do one of them, as I had a friend in that particular city. I'd hoped she'd help me out, picking me up at the airport, getting me to the hotel, making it easy on me since I still couldn't lift anything heavier than a gallon of milk with my left arm. But instead she let me know that I'd have to figure out how to get to and from the airport on my own, which had me in tears. I told Ed that was a sign, and I should stay home. Fortunately, the event's organizers were very understanding when I bowed out.

I didn't travel out of state until late March of 2007, a week after finishing radiation therapy. The left side of my chest had turned a deep red with white bubbles beneath my skin. Though I didn't peel, the area was very sensitive. "You came through with flying colors," Dr. G insisted, and I was just so thankful to be done.

Still, I was fearful as I packed my bag to travel to San Antonio for the Texas Library Association's annual convention. Ed accompanied me, and he was great about lifting my suitcase and making sure I was in the window seat so no one could bump my left side. Once we were there, it was a lovely experience. I felt so supported by the loud applause at the mystery dinner that first night, and the next morning, the amazing librarians lined up at the HarperCollins booth as I signed copies of *The Lone Star Lonely Hearts Club*. I came away from TLA feeling like a rock star. It was just the mental boost I needed.

My next trip was to Houston for the Romantic Times' Booklovers Convention without Ed by my side. The worst part of it was asking the flight attendant if she could help me get my carry-on into the overhead rack. "I've just gone through breast cancer surgery and radiation treatment, and I can't lift anything heavier than a milk jug," I confessed.

Instead of being gracious and giving me a hand, she scowled and said, "If you can't lift the bag overhead, you'll have to go back to the gate and check it."

Seriously? I would have broken down and cried if not for a gentleman in a nearby seat who jumped up and said, "I'll put that in the bin for you."

I appreciated his kindness more than he would ever know.

The Houston trip otherwise went off without a hitch. I saw lots of friends at the convention who were relieved that I was getting around so well. It was a nice diversion, but I was incredibly glad to get home.

Though I had pared down my obligations in order to take better care of myself—and had turned in *Too Pretty to Die*, about a month late—I still had my *Debs* deadline to meet and a wedding to plan. Ed and I had decided to get married on February 24, 2008, slightly less than a year away, and I wanted to be fit and healthy when we said, "I do." Once I got clearance from Dr. O, I found a local trainer who was sympathetic to my plight and tailored workouts so I could slowly regain strength and tone without jeopardizing my recovery. I only saw her once or twice a week and, in between, I used my treadmill, my exercise ball, and my hand weights to gradually build up my endurance.

It took endurance of another kind entirely to be my own wedding planner, but it was something I wanted to do. I felt like this wedding was more than a celebration of our commitment. It was a celebration of life and survival, of the loved ones who'd supported us during a very tough ordeal. Maybe that was why pink played an important part in our color scheme. It symbolized my breast cancer fight. I even considered having a wedding dress made by a designer who sewed pink ribbons inside the skirt; but that didn't pan out. Instead, I found a very simple but elegant ivory dress while shopping with my mother. The seamstress who did the alterations sewed cups into the ruched bodice so I didn't have to wear a bra (ah, that was lovely!).

Soon, the florist was hired, the invitations ordered, the caterer selected, and deposits handed over for the venues for ceremony and reception. I managed to get through a messy first draft of *The Debs* and worked like crazy on the revision notes my Random House editor sent (luckily, the revisions on *Too Pretty to Die* for Avon were minimal—whew!).

I went in for boob checks every three months and sometimes in between, like when a few miles on the treadmill caused Frankenboob to turn rainbow colors again. Even months and months after radiation therapy, my skin and tissue were supersensitive. Dr. G wasn't sure why that had happened but she had her nurse take pictures, and I imagined my multicolored boob as part of a Power Point presentation, shown on a large screen at some radiology convention for hundreds of white coats to see.

Before I knew it, summer had turned into fall and then the holidays were upon us. I finally felt as though the worst was over. My wedding would take place in a few short months, and Ed and I would start a new phase in our lives, one I envisioned as filled with good health and the hopes of a baby.

Then I heard from my mother that my aunt Mary had been diagnosed with bilateral breast cancer. Just as I was on the path to regaining my health, Mary's fight was only beginning. And her diagnosis would not be the last for the women in my family.

In October of 2010 as I was planning a fund-raiser and toiling away on my second women's fiction title, *Little Black Dress*, I would not only find out that I was pregnant—surprise!—but my mother would show up on my doorstep, telling me she had cancer as well.

. . . And a Baby

Chapter Seven

Feast or famine.

WHEN I WAS in high school, my mom would often say, "It's either feast or famine." I either had several boys pursuing me or no one interested at all. In those days, I much preferred the "feast." As I got older, however, I thought of that saying in terms of life in general. It seemed like I either had way too much on my plate or very little, and I began to realize how wonderful it was when "famine" set in. Those were the calm times, the days when I could get everything done and still had time to breathe. It was the feasts that scared me as they always came so unexpectedly, often dumping both the bad and good into my lap at once; shattering any peace I'd found and filling my world with stress.

The fall of 2010 was definitely a time of feast, a smorgasbord laden with plenty of good and bad. For one, I was working hard on my second women's fiction book to follow *The Cougar Club*. Called *Little Black Dress*, it centered on two very different sisters and a magical black dress that would tear them apart. The story felt very personal as my sister and I are about as different as two people can be. The way she lives her life tends to tie my stomach in knots. While composing the novel, I was more emotional than usual, which I attributed to the fact that I was also spearheading my first fund-raiser, Wine, Wit & Lit, which brought together authors, wine, and baskets for silent auction and raffle in order to raise funds for a nonprofit called Casting for Recovery that supports breast cancer survivors.

When I described my weepiness, fatigue, and upset stomach to my mother, she showed up with a pregnancy test kit from the drugstore. I only realized then that I'd missed my last period. So as Mom sat in the bedroom and waited, I took the test . . . and it was positive! I was forty-six, a breast cancer survivor of four years, and I had a tiny bun in the oven! It was a dream come true, and not only for me. My mother practically bounced off the walls, and Ed was equally excited when I told him about the baby.

So added to my book deadline and the breast cancer fundraiser was a surprise pregnancy. Feast enough, you say?

How I wish that had been all that dropped on my plate, but the universe had more in store for me yet.

Our baby cat, Blue, the youngest of our three felines, suddenly came down with a type of hemolytic anemia, where her immune system was attacking and destroying her red blood cells. When we realized something was wrong, she was already jaundiced. Our vet immediately sent us to the emergency animal clinic, which scheduled a blood transfusion. We were told she only had a fifty-fifty chance of survival and would likely not make it through the next forty-eight hours.

So there I was, terrified that our sweet Blue might not live; worried about my newfound pregnancy as I had some early spotting that scared me; determined to carry on with the breast cancer fund-raiser; writing a book that drained me emotionally; and then another shoe dropped.

My mom showed up at my doorstep unexpectedly one day, looking extremely anxious. Before she'd even gotten all the way into the house, she blurted out, "I have breast cancer."

The news floored me, mostly because she had told me nothing about having a suspicious mammogram or undergoing a core biopsy. "I didn't want to worry you," she said. "You have enough going on."

But that's what daughters are for!

Oy!

Blunt as my mother has always been, she tends to be guarded with her emotions and awfully secretive when it comes to health scares. I realized since my diagnosis and Aunt Mary's that she'd been extra-concerned about her own breast health, but she'd been there for me while I went through my scare. Was it selfish that I wished I could have been there for her when she was getting her bad news?

At least I knew what to do. I didn't bawl or need references for breast surgeons. "We're calling Dr. O's office first thing in the morning," I told her. "We'll get you in for a consultation and then we'll proceed from there."

I found this page in a notebook that I wrote while sitting in the waiting room at the breast center, which describes my feelings the day of her appointment:

09/21/10

    This time, when Mom picks me up, it's for her
    appointment with Dr. O, not mine (tho' I have a
    follow-up and mammo a week from today).

    I'm holding her mammogram films that show
    the density and the copies of her core needle biopsy
    results. "Known malignancy," they say
    (I peeked).

    There are path slides in a padded envelope. I'm
    not messing with those.

    Seems so weird to think, almost four years ago, I
    was the one with the "known malignancy." I was the
    patient, not she.

    Strange how life comes full circle sometimes.

    I am calm though, knowing they caught it early.
    But I'm still anxious about what Dr. O will say.

It was an odd juxtaposition, being the daughter yet having been the one who went through something first. Being able to reassure her and answer any of her questions.

I felt like a hostess that day at the breast center, introducing her to the doctors and medical team that had taken care of me. Instead of tears, there were hugs and smiles. Everyone assured me that they'd take great care of my mother, just as they had me, and I knew they would. Mom's cancer had been caught very, very early. It was no larger than a pea. It was not aggressive. At seventy-three years old, she would not be thrown into more treatment than she needed. The most conservative road would be the one taken.

While my aunt had undergone bilateral mastectomy, chemo, and radiation as well as multiple reconstructive surgeries, and I had undergone lumpectomy, re-excision, and thirty-four sessions of radiation; my mother would need only lumpectomy and seventeen sessions of radiation.

"That's baby stuff," I told her. "You are going to be just fine."

My sister—the one who's night to my day—was able to fly down to St. Louis to play nurse to my mother while I dealt with my deadline, my fund-raiser (which, of course, was set for the weekend following Mom's surgery), and my sick cat, Blue (to whom Ed played nurse, dispensing pills and liquid steroids twice a day!).

Soon enough, the feast became less of a buffet and more like a Weight Watchers dinner. My mom would be good as new. Blue would survive her brush with death. My deadline would be met. The fund-raiser would raise enough money to send a survivor and a half to the Casting for Recovery fly-fishing retreat.

What was left on the menu was my pregnancy, only that wasn't going well at all.

By seven weeks, the ultrasound did not show a fetal heartbeat. In fact, while they'd found a fetal pole on the previous scan, they couldn't even find the fetus now. The radiologist who popped in during that dismal ultrasound rattled on about calling my doctor and considering a D&C. I didn't want to accept that the pregnancy wasn't viable. It was the day before Christmas Eve of 2010. Just four years earlier on Christmas Eve, Ed had proposed to me; and days after that, I had my lumpectomy. By God, I did not want the holidays to be filled with sadness again!

I prayed that the radiologist was wrong. I didn't want a D&C. If this baby wasn't meant to be, I wanted my body to take care of it on its own.

As it turned out, no amount of prayers could save the pregnancy. Over New Year's weekend of 2011, I suffered a miscarriage. It was tragic and horribly painful and one of the most awful things I've ever been through in my life.

It was enough to make me stop believing in miracles. I nearly gave up on the idea that Ed and I would have a baby before I was too old and all my eggs had dried up.

Even though my doctor informed me, "You'll be more fertile for the next two years so keep trying," I kept thinking, *But I'm already forty-six. How fertile can I be at this point?*

Apparently, fertile enough.

Chapter Eight

There are two pink lines!

•

I BURIED MYSELF in my writing, so thankful that I had so many deadlines in 2011; although revising *Little Black Dress* during the first few months of the year wasn't easy. One of the characters suffers a miscarriage in the story, and that hit awfully close to home. As I rewrote the book, I cried off and on, figuring it was good to let it out. My hormones were slowly coming down from the pregnancy, getting back to normal, and life was moving on.

By mid-spring, I had turned in the final version of *Little Black Dress* to my editor at HarperCollins and had my proposal accepted for my next women's fiction book. That one started out being called *Little White Lies* but soon became *The Truth About Love and Lightning*. Because of crazy scheduling, I had to put *Love and Lightning* on the back burner for a bit and start work on a young adult thriller for Delacorte. It was a nice change of pace, and I had fun slipping into mystery author mode again. By July, I had a rough draft of the thriller done and I'd begun *Love and Lightning*, which focuses on a mother who can't tell anything but the brutal truth and a daughter who can't help but lie.

The novel also involves an unexpected late-in-life pregnancy, perhaps some wishful thinking on my part. It was good for my psyche to create a character who gets to have something I so recently lost.

While I toiled on *Love and Lightning*, I also got busy promoting the release of *Little Black Dress* in late August of 2011. It was incredibly easy to talk up that tale with readers, as it was truly a book of my heart. I had a handful of local gigs lined up for St. Louis, including a fund-raiser at Saks Fifth Avenue with the St. Louis affiliate of Susan G. Komen for the Cure, for which I'd done several events since my breast cancer treatment. I love combining "books and boobs" whenever it works out. Additionally, my publisher sent me on the road, speaking and signing books at several trade shows in September.

And I found myself agreeing to put on a second Wine, Wit & Lit fund-raiser for Casting for Recovery in late October. That would be my last event of the fall so I could hunker down to finish *Love and Lightning*.

I was feeling good about my health and positive about the

direction of my career and the books I was writing. I even mentioned to Ed that I wanted to do more fund-raising and volunteering as I needed "something more" in my life that felt equally fulfilling.

In the meantime, my forty-seventh birthday rolled around in mid-October, and we celebrated by going out to lunch with family and then heading to Pumpkin Land to shoot the corn cannons, wander through the corn maze, and pick out Halloween pumpkins. I had a huge berry margarita at the Mexican restaurant that afternoon, although it tasted really weak. I'm such a lightweight that usually a drink that big will make me loopy. This one didn't (luckily).

It was a beautiful Sunday with a picture-perfect blue sky. Ed and I had spent a few hours at Pumpkin Land, acting like kids and having a blast. We left with two pumpkins and big smiles on our faces.

The next day, as I procrastinated getting to the computer, I began cleaning out my bathroom vanity (it's amazing how much laundry gets done and how often the rugs get vacuumed when I'm on deadline!). I happened upon a single pregnancy test stick left in an otherwise empty box, and I briefly considered just trashing it all.

Instead, I decided to use it, and not because of intuition or a premonition or a gut feeling (although that would make for a better story!). It was one of those what-the-heck? moments. I didn't have any pregnancy symptoms. I'd just gotten my period about three weeks before, as a matter of fact. So I had no expectations whatsoever. I guess I was ever-hopeful, having done the tests periodically during the ten months since my miscarriage. I kept praying I'd see a plus sign again. But so far that hadn't happened.

So imagine my surprise when I took the test and saw two pink lines appear in the tiny window. *Holy cow!* I was pregnant!

Flabbergasted, I initially questioned if the test was expired or had malfunctioned somehow. There was a warning on the instructions noting something like "Women over forty may have a false positive reading due to fluky hormones."

Not sure how to react, I called my mother, who was as shocked as I was. "Don't tell Ed, especially while he's at work," she advised, not wanting me to get his hopes up.

But that was the very next thing I did.

I phoned his cell, which he answered with a hushed "Yeah?"

"Are you in a meeting?" I asked.

"Yes," he whispered.

My heart thumping, I blurted out, "I peed on a stick, and there are two pink lines!"

"What?"

So I repeated what I'd told him, saying, "I think I'm pregnant."

He was so quiet that I wondered if he'd fallen off his chair and had to be revived.

The next thing I did was buy another box of test sticks, a different brand this time. If I was pregnant, it was so early that I figured maybe other tests would show different results.

Only all the tests were positive.

I bought every kind of pregnancy test on the market and, over the course of the next few weeks, I used them all.

Every single one said "pregnant."

I lined them all up on my toilet tank and stared at them day after day until the pink lines and plus signs slowly faded. I was too afraid to call my doctor's office until I was sure I was at least seven weeks along. I didn't want to go through what I'd gone through before: heading to the lab every other day for blood tests to measure my hormone levels, which never seemed to increase enough, and enduring ultrasounds that were disappointing from the get-go.

Even before I saw my doctor, I started prenatal vitamins and read every article available on having a healthy first trimester. I stopped drinking green tea (it supposedly prevents folic acid from binding). I quit taking the lysine supplement I'd been using daily to help boost my immune system, which I'd felt the radiation had compromised (there's not enough data about lysine's effects on pregnancy so it's safer to avoid it). I also ate as many fruits and veggies as possible despite the frequent bouts of nausea.

At eight weeks, I phoned my gynecologist and agreed to have a blood test. Happily, the results this time were anything but marginal. My HCG level was through the roof at just under 150,000. "This is a *good* pregnancy," my doctor told us at our appointment, and we saw a heartbeat on the very first ultrasound, something we'd never had the chance to see before. Ed and I were holding hands, laughing and crying at the same time. It was so amazing that it was surreal!

Before we left the doctor's office, we were handed the official packet for mothers-to-be, chock-full of information, which is when I knew everything was different. We hadn't been given The Packet the last time around.

As great as things looked, I couldn't help but be nervous. I'd read the statistics that said less than one percent of women over forty-five could get pregnant with their own eggs, so I knew I'd beaten the odds again (kind of like falling in love with Ed and getting married when I was over forty as opposed to being killed by a terrorist). This pregnancy was unbelievably precious, and I did not want to suffer another loss if I could help it.

Ed and I waited to share the news with family and close friends until we reached eleven weeks and had another good ultrasound. We put off telling the rest of the world for two weeks more until I was safely through the first trimester.

Not surprisingly, the baby was all I could think about. My energy focused on this new life inside me, nearly to the exclusion of everything else. I had trouble concentrating on *The Truth About Love and Lightning*. Every blog I wrote and every Facebook post was about this miraculous bun in the oven. I noticed each tiny change as the months went along: the growing curve of my belly, the nausea, the exhaustion interspersed with bursts of energy, the way I began to huff and puff going up and down the stairs.

I developed a skin rash in the second trimester that drove me insane. My dermatologist diagnosed "pruritis of pregnancy," which normally doesn't show up until the third trimester. But, you know, I just love standing out from the crowd. I tried to deal with the rash without a prescription, until it went on for over a month. Every piece of clothing irritated me. Lying down in bed was uncomfortable. Sitting up was uncomfortable. After about six weeks of misery that lasted through the Christmas holidays, Ed found me in the bathroom in the middle of the night, witch hazel–soaked Kleenex all over my arms, legs, and chest. I was sobbing, saying, "I can't take it anymore," which is when I caved and told the dermatologist, "I'll take the steroids!" Two weeks on a tapering dose of prednisone, and the rash was gone, never to be seen again (hallelujah!).

Though sometimes I wish I'd caved sooner, I like to tell myself that I gave my baby six weeks to grow without any medication interfering with her development.

We had the fetal anatomy scan in early February, not long after I finished my course of steroids. I was beyond excited to see the baby on the big monitors at the hospital's wellness center; but I was nervous, too, because the scan is very thorough and can often take an hour to complete. There's a huge checklist they go through, looking at baby's skull, brain, chest, heart, lungs, etc. They search for the most subtle of abnormalities, such as the thickness of the nuchal fold at the back of the neck, which could indicate Down syndrome.

I wondered if being an older mother would cause any problems for the baby. All my blood tests had been great. I knew I was in good shape and had done everything I could to ensure this was a healthy pregnancy. But there are no guarantees in life, as I kept learning time and again. Still, Ed and I had decided that we would accept whatever God gave us. We loved this baby already. We could deal with the rest.

The tech was also able to discern the sex of the child, something Ed and I really wanted to know. My mother had been confident from the beginning that the baby was a boy. I had ordered an over-the-counter "gender test" that had suggested the baby was a girl. So we were curious which was right.

The ultrasound pictures were incredible. We were used to the grainy images in my doctor's office, but this equipment was much sharper and we were able to see more of the baby at once. We marveled at her beautifully formed skull, her spine and ribs, and her incredible beating heart. We even saw her little hands and feet! And, yes, I say "her," because the tech pointed out the "three lines" (also known as "the hamburger") that proved she was a girl.

We already had a name for her: Emily Alice, because I'd always loved the name Emily, and Alice is Ed's mom.

Both mothers were invited into the exam room at the end of the scan so they could see their granddaughter for themselves. It was a wonderful moment, a real gift. This was it, I realized then, the "something more" that I'd been looking for. I was going to be a mom!

Nothing could have dampened my mood at that point, not even the radiologist popping in to see Ed and me before we left and reminding us that we hadn't done an amniocentesis so we couldn't be sure if there were chromosomal abnormalities. (This was the same doctor who'd suggested no hope with the last pregnancy, for which I'd dubbed him Dr. Doom. Hey, if the nickname fits . . .)

Except for a brief stint in a hyperbaric chamber after our old furnace leaked carbon monoxide in the middle of the night, I suffered only typical side effects of pregnancy: peeing a lot, swollen ankles and feet, bloody rhinitis. Though some days were better than others, I felt pretty good throughout and was energetic enough to tackle my editor's revision notes for *The Truth About Love and Lightning* in about a month. Is it bragging to say I'm so proud of that story? The book exceeded my expectations on so many levels, particularly since I wondered if it would even be coherent, considering all that had been going on while I'd written it. My editor seemed equally in love, which made me pleased as Punch.

Once *Love and Lightning* was headed to the copy editor, I'd hoped to get a little time off to relax and concentrate on Emily's arrival; but apparently there is no rest for the weary. At nine months' pregnant, I began writing *In the Pink*. I couldn't put it off for fear that Emily would make her debut before I'd had a chance to finish.

As I sit here now, pounding away at the keyboard with tingling fingers (thanks to pregnancy-fueled carpal tunnel), I'm so large that I can't pull my chair up to my desk. I have to sit back a ways and balance my puffy feet on a stool underneath. But even the discomfort is worth it. I've never written any kind of memoir before, just snippets of past events for blogs or articles. Dipping back into the last seven years has been quite an emotional roller-coaster.

I'm proud of how much I've done since I turned forty, how thoroughly I've lived my life, going through the best of times and the worst of times in equal measures.

I've come to understand the true definition of the word "courage": facing something frightening and pushing through it. It doesn't mean you aren't scared. It simply means you do what you must to survive, taking each step one at a time. And when you have doubts that you're not up to the task, you consider the women who've done it before you and who will do it after you. They're heroes, every single one of them.

Being told you have cancer is terrifying and changes us forever in ways we could never imagine. The scars it leaves on our bodies aren't nearly as deep as the ones carved into our minds. As another survivor once sarcastically remarked, "Cancer is the gift that keeps on giving." The memories of what we've been through—the physical aches and pains—will never vanish entirely; but, hopefully, they will make us stronger and wiser, and cause us to appreciate our lives all the more.

No matter what fate throws at us, we should never forget that there is *always* hope.

There is always room for love and happiness and, yes, miracles.

If you ever need proof that miracles do exist, just think of this forty-seven-year-old survivor giving birth to her first child. That's the beauty of life, isn't it? Anything can happen. We just have to stick around long enough to see what's next.

IN THE PINK
Q&A with Susan McBride

(1) How do you feel now about the doctor who diagnosed your cancer as a cyst?

I adore her. She's been my doctor for about sixteen years, and I can't imagine ever leaving her care. My rare type of cancer (pure mucinous carcinoma) manifests as a blob of mucus with cells trapped inside. As I mentioned in the book, the pathology showed a benign growth on the tumor. So here's how I look at it: if my doctor had not felt this "cyst" on exam and alerted me to its existence, I never would have focused on that breast and followed up the way I did. What if there had been no palpable growth in conjunction with the negative mammogram? I might not have found my cancer until it was much bigger and more frightening. So I credit my doctor with alerting me to a situation I otherwise would have ignored because I was so busy at the time. I am forever grateful, too, that I followed my own instincts and pursued an answer rather than just letting things go.

(2) What about the doctor who insisted on chemo?

I stopped seeing her a few years past my treatment. She and I just did not click. And it's true that my blood pressure went up every time I had an appointment with her. I know other patients who think she's great and she's well respected by the medical community. So this was absolutely a case of patient and doctor not connecting.

(3) The man on the plane who helped lift your bags couldn't have come to your aid at a better time. Were there other instances in which you were saved by the kindness of strangers, or surprised by their apathy?

Thank goodness, most folks I encountered were as kind as could be, unlike the rude flight attendant. The loveliest surprise came when other authors I knew—or in some cases, hadn't known before—heard about my situation and got in touch to share their stories, offer advice, and cheer me on. These were women who'd been very private about their own treatment (and still are); but their reaching out helped sustain me through my treatment. I consider them angels who appeared right when I needed them and I will always think fondly of each. I also heard from complete strangers who offered hope and inspiration, who sent homemade quilts, stuffed animals, and cards. It still amazes me to recall all the incredible displays of generosity. I will remember those acts of kindness for as long as I live.

(4) Could you give us an update on your mother and aunt?

My mom is her usual dynamic self almost two years postdiagnosis. She still has some aches and pains in her left breast (did I mention that we both were diagnosed in our left boobs?), but that's a common side effect of surgery and radiation. Every once in a while if she worries about a bump or pain, I urge her to see Dr. O, which she does without hesitation. Mom is like the Energizer Bunny. You would never know she'd been through anything at all without her bringing it up.

Nearly five years post her diagnosis, my aunt is as dynamic as ever (she lives out of state but I saw her in January for my mom's seventy-fifth birthday). She's back to all her social and charitable endeavors and her frequent travels. She has gone through multiple surgeries and had a successful reconstruction on one of her breasts. Things didn't pan out quite as she'd hoped with the other breast. So she calls them Barbie and Ken, and she likes to say that it's no surprise Ken has been the bigger pain in the ass. With her blessing, I share that tidbit when I speak at breast cancer fund-raisers. People seem to get a kick out of it!

(5) What advice would you give to friends and families of those going through cancer treatment? How can we help our loved ones to heal?

Be supportive in whatever way you can, even if it's making a phone call or shooting off e-mails now and then just to ask, "How're you doing?" Understand the range of emotions that come with someone being diagnosed and don't ever belittle feelings of helplessness or fear. Let your loved one know she has the right to be scared and even to throw a pity party now and then. Just don't let those pity parties go on for too long! If you feel inclined to give gifts, make them gifts of comfort, like fuzzy socks, a soft throw, favorite movies or TV shows on DVD. Keep up a sense of humor. Laughter is great medicine. Realize that this isn't a process that's neatly wrapped up in a week, or even months. The healing process takes years, maybe a lifetime. So don't tell a survivor to "snap out of it" or you might get smacked upside the head. Be patient and listen. Sometimes advice isn't needed as much as a shoulder to lean on.

(6) Have you met new friends because of having cancer that you might not otherwise have made? Do you feel as if the bond with other survivors is stronger than that with your friends who haven't dealt with cancer?

I have definitely made friends because of my diagnosis that I would not have made otherwise, like Helen Chesnut, the executive director of the St. Louis affiliate of Susan G. Komen for the Cure, and Patti Hummert, the Missouri coordinator of Casting for Recovery. They both make me laugh and inspire me, and I'm glad every day that I know them. I've become friendly with a number of survivors online and from the speaking I've done. Survivors do have a special connection. We can talk about things that we don't talk about with those who haven't been through what we've been through. It's very liberating. It's been interesting with my mom having gone through breast cancer as well. Being able to share such a strange and life-changing experience is like sharing a secret, one that adds a different depth to the relationship.

(7) Do you have a way of memorializing your years since kicking cancer?

I'm heading toward six years since my diagnosis this December (2012). I think there's always a moment every year on December 28 when I look at Ed or my mom and say, "Can you believe I was having my first surgery on this date in 2006?" Or every January 10 when I remember going back in for my re-excision. I don't imagine I'll ever forget those anniversaries. But I don't do anything big or special. I truly celebrate each and every day. I am happy to wake up each morning and be able to write the books I want to write. And I feel like the luckiest woman alive every time I see Ed smile or ponder the miracle that is Emily. In fact, speaking of Emily, she was born in late June under the sign of Cancer, which I find kind of funny. It's like the universe is saying, *See! There's a positive side to that word after all. Embrace it!* Every day that I'm healthy is a celebration. So is talking about what happened to me and causing someone else who's diagnosed to think, *If she can do it, I can do it.* That's something to cheer!

Susan's Tips on Dating After Forty

1. Let trusted friends set you up rather than looking for love online. Yeah, I know, maybe it's my age but I still don't trust strangers over the Internet (or Web sites that require too much personal information—they can get hacked)! I like meeting people face-to-face from the get-go. You'll get more immediate and truthful reactions one-on-one than you ever will from a text, e-mail, Facebook comment, or tweet. **And if you don't have friends who'll set you up, get out there and *do* things where you'll meet new people**. Take that art class you've been putting off, sign up for tai chi, learn a new language, or join a bird-watching group. Seriously, if you're doing something you enjoy and you meet someone else who enjoys the same thing, you're already ahead of the game.

2. Be your authentic self; but be your *best* self. Here's where you take a look at yourself and decide if there's room for improvement. Have you been slacking in the exercise department? Are you drinking scads of soda and eating too much fast food? I'm not saying that you have to be lean and mean and ready to tackle a marathon. But I want you to feel fit and healthy and strong. If you love yourself, you'll take care of yourself by consuming food that's good for you and keeping your muscles (especially that heart muscle!) fit. Also, look at your hair and wardrobe. Have you not tweaked your appearance since 1988? I had the same "boring bob" for at least twenty years before I let it go. Even doing something as simple as getting a new cut or color—or a couple of fresh outfits that are outside your comfort zone—can be inspiring. However, if you decide to make some changes, do it for yourself, not for anyone else.

3. Don't look at every date as an attempt to find a potential mate. Look at dates as a chance to make new friends. I think we set ourselves up for failure when we invest too much in a first or second date with someone new. If you put less pressure on yourself, you'll have more fun and you'll be less nervous. Try meeting for lunch or coffee at a bookstore instead of dinner. And remember, if you arrive in your own car, you can leave at will. Sometimes you won't feel sparks fly right away either. I think the best relationships—and the longest lasting—begin as friendships first. So don't give up on someone you genuinely like and have a lot in common with if you don't feel lust at first sight.

4. Listen to your gut. If warning bells go off about anything—and I mean *anything*—take a hint. There are reasons that we have instincts. They're for survival. If your inner

voice tells you this person isn't kosher, if you sense any threat
or danger, if you just get a weird vibe but you don't know why,
pay attention. When it comes to relationships, as with our
health, we need to acknowledge that gut feeling and realize
that it's often right.

5. If at first you don't succeed, try, try again. Before I met
Ed, I met more than a few men who were completely wrong
for me (ah, let me count the ways!). If you realize you've made
a mistake, don't let that derail you forever. Everyone has
lapses in judgment. Don't blame yourself if a new relationship
does not work. Some things are just not meant to be. When
you find the right person—the one who accepts you and loves
you for who you are—you will feel it to your bones! Bad relationships are worse than no relationships. If all cylinders
aren't clicking, move on.

6. Be kind to yourself and realize that *it's okay to be alone*.
I know too many women who've gotten involved in really
bad relationships just so they don't have to stay home and
watch TV or read a book on a Saturday night. I'm not sure
what's wrong with staying home and reading, to be honest!
If you can't stand to be by yourself, maybe you need to find
out why. The best mates are folks who feel complete and who
don't depend on someone else to entertain them or give them
worth. Single people can have wonderful, full lives with ca-
reers, hobbies, friends, and family. If you are happy and content, you will attract people who are happy and content. If
you are miserable and insecure, you will attract folks who are

miserable and insecure or who prey on those who are miserable and insecure. You must learn to love yourself before you can fully love someone else.

7. Life is short, so enjoy every moment. Don't wait until a health crisis to stop and smell the roses. It's okay to say no to others once in a while. Save some time for yourself. Make sure you're doing at least one thing you love every day, even if it's waking up to see the sun rise, taking a bubble bath, or sipping tea on the patio. Live simply and understand that the little things *are* important.

What I Learned from My Diagnosis

1. Take Control of Your Health Care and Be Your Own Advocate.

Cancer can happen to anyone at any age. I wasn't a drinker or smoker. I was never considered overweight. Initially, there was no indication in my family history that I was more susceptible than the average Jane. Sometimes there is no concrete answer as to why bad things happen. That's just life. What's important when you're dealing with something tricky like cancer is to catch it early. If you're a woman, that means *having annual physical exams and screening tests like mammograms.* You can't just do these things willy-nilly. Especially once you hit forty, you need to pay attention to what's going on with your body. I've had several fortysomething moms tell me, "Oh, I haven't had a mammogram in years! Guess I should probably get one, huh?" I have to refrain from slapping them silly. If you don't do these things for yourself and you're a mom, do them for your kids so they have their mother around for a long, long time.

Get copies of your lab work and become familiar with what your numbers are and mean. Keep a file for your medical records. Doctors have lots of patients, and sometimes patients see lots of doctors. You need to be the one in control of your medical information. You need to stay on top of things. Don't rely on someone else to take charge for you. This is even more important when you're diagnosed with a serious illness.

Be proactive, ask questions, and learn as much as you can about what you're dealing with. And if you're too frightened or paralyzed to be your own best advocate, ask a friend or family member who's pushy/bossy to be your spokesperson. You are not a sheep. You are not a statistic. You're a unique individual who deserves to be treated as such. The medical treatment that works for someone else may not work for you. You need to pay attention and be informed so that the decisions you make are ones you can live with for the rest of your life.

2. Doctors Are Not Dictators—You Are in the Driver's Seat.

Yes, you must trust your doctor. Yes, you must have enough faith to believe that she knows what she's doing and is looking out for your best interests. But that doesn't mean you should blindly accept and do everything she says. (See be your own advocate, above!) *Your course of treatment is up to you in the end.* Your doctor should give you options and explain them thoroughly. Although time is of the essence, you should still take a deep breath and make sure you understand your choices. Think them over and speak with your loved ones before you proceed. Once I had learned as much as I could about my particular rare cancer from trusted medical sites online and from research studies I looked up, I felt competent to ask more in-depth questions and to challenge certain aspects of my proposed treatment. My oncologist was bound and determined that I have chemo. But when I read my pathology report (something every patient *should* read and understand) and numerous articles on pure mucinous carcinoma, I felt that chemotherapy would be overkill. I discussed this with all of my doctors independently, and a majority agreed (three out of four, as a matter of fact). Thus, I felt very comfortable saying, "No, thank you. I will do the six and a half weeks of radiation therapy but I will pass on the chemo cocktail." It gave me a sense of control to actually have a say in things.

Every patient needs to feel that sense of participation in and acceptance of her treatment. Again, we need to trust our doctors (and, if we don't, we need to find new physicians); but we also *must* arm ourselves with knowledge, ask questions, and take an active part in choosing the correct path for our individual needs.

3. There Are Things You Will Learn Only from Going Through Them.

I wish I could tell you that modern medicine had all the answers; that, once you're diagnosed, you'll get all pertinent facts about what you'll be facing, every ache and pain and weird twinge. But that won't be the case. *There were many side effects of my treatment that I only found out about by going through them.* And often when I asked my medical team about the odd sensations I experienced, they could not give me answers. I learned more about what was "normal" from other survivors than I did from my doctors or nurses. In fact, when I went to my thirty-four sessions of radiation, one of my goals was to chat with the women in the waiting room, find out their situations, and ask at least one question, like "Did you ever wake up in the middle of the night with shooting pains in your chest like you were having a heart attack?" Answer: "Yes." It was *so* nice to know I wasn't alone or actually having a heart attack.

Know that your surgery and treatment will affect your body (and your mind) for years to come. I have aching ribs in my radiation treatment area when rain is coming (yes, like arthritis). I have had stabbing pains that I've attributed to the fact that the heart muscle and muscles nearby are often touched by the radiation. Surgery clips nerves that may never recover properly or recover at all. Many survivors have no sensation under their armpits after node removal. Be accepting that whatever was done has been done to keep you healthy and alive for as long as possible; but understand that you are not the same person as you were before. You've had trauma to your skin, nerves, muscles, etc. Your true recovery will be years in coming, and your mind won't ever completely reset to where you were before your diagnosis. However, you will adapt. You will be stronger for it. You will move on.

4. Embrace All Those Follow-up Appointments.

For at least five years following your diagnosis, you will see your doctors *a lot*. I think I was going in every three months to see someone on my team, if only for a breast exam. Okay, yes, it sounds like a pain, but it's important to stay on top of your recovery. I always found these follow-ups reassuring. I did eventually stop seeing my radiation oncologist (whom I adored) and my oncologist (I found her very dismissive of the positive changes I'd made in my life, like eating organic, switching to more natural and organic products for my body and my house.). But I still see my breast surgeon twice a year as I alternate a mammogram with an ultrasound every six months (and she reviews all pictures with the radiologist immediately before she sees me for a physical exam in her office). I still have an MRI of my breasts every two years as well. I also don't hesitate to call and schedule an appointment if something doesn't look or feel right. In fact, during my recent pregnancy I went in because my left breast turned bright red after I worked in the yard in an ill-fitting exercise bra. Honestly, I'd rather look like a worrywart than say, "Aw, I'm sure it's nothing," and I would urge all women to do the same. *It is far, far better to be safe than sorry.*

Additional Information

For additional information, please visit these Web sites:

http://SusanMcBride.com
http://HopkinsMedicine.org
http://MayoClinic.com
http://BreastCancer.org
http://Komen.org
http://CastingforRecovery.org
http://LiveStrong.org

An excerpt from

The Truth About Love and Lightning

Available February 2013 from
William Morrow Paperbacks

Prologue

ANNIKA BRINK COULD not tell a lie.

From as far back as Gretchen could remember, her mother had been unable to utter anything but the cold, unvarnished truth—or, at least, the truth according to Annika—and, as Gretchen learned quickly enough as a child, often the truth set no one free and was downright painful besides.

As when the twins were born when Gretchen was five. "They are not right," Annika had insisted, her pale hair wild and hands on her hips, such a ferocious frown on her lips that it looked for all intents and purposes as though she might want to take them back to the county hospital posthaste.

Which had Gretchen wondering if one could return babies the same way one returned a glass bottle drained of soda to the grocer's for a nickel.

"Do you not see what I see?" Annika had nagged her very tolerant husband.

"They look fine to me," Gretchen's father had replied, and he'd bent over the double-wide crib to first rub Bennie's belly and then Trudy's. "They've each got ten fingers and ten toes, perfect button noses, and ears like tiny seashells."

"Then you are as blind as they are," Annika had bluntly stated. "Look at their eyes! They're such a milky blue and neither so much as blinks when I pass my hand before them. Do you think it's my fault, for painting while I was pregnant?" she had asked, madly pacing. "Was it the fumes from the oils or the turpentine? As an artist, I can't imagine a more horrible curse than to lose one's sight!"

"Oh, I can think of plenty," Gretchen's father had coolly replied, his knuckles turning white as he gripped the crib's railing. "Would you cast out a calf because it couldn't see, when its milk will be no different than a cow with sight?"

"Please!" Annika had loudly and dismissively snorted. "I know you believe animals are like people because you spend more time with beasts than humans," she'd told him, "but these are our daughters, not barnyard creatures!"

For a long moment, Gretchen had shut out their voices, having heard them argue enough before about her father's job as a farm veterinarian, how it kept them in Walnut Ridge when Annika found so much about small-town life uncultured and unfit.

Instead, she had crept toward the bars of the crib and peered through as if staring at a pair of sleeping monkeys at the zoo. If there was something wrong with her new sisters, she couldn't see it from where she stood.

"C'mon, Anni, enough." Her father had expelled a weary

sigh. "Nothing's your fault. Nothing's anyone's fault. Sometimes things just happen, and no one's to blame. If it's not life or death, we'll get through it."

"They will never have normal lives."

"Normal is overrated," he'd declared, shaking his head. It was a minute before he seemed to realize Gretchen was there beside him, her upturned face full of worry. "Better to be different, don't you think, sweet pea?" he had said, his voice suddenly lighter as he ruffled her bright yellow curls. "That's how you make your mark. Not by being the same as everyone else."

But Gretchen had not agreed. Her mother's words had her frightened.

"What will happen to them?" she'd asked, and had slipped a small hand through the crib rails to poke tiny Trudy. She was no bigger than a pot roast, although pot roasts didn't drool in their sleep. "We'll keep them, won't we?"

"Of course we'll keep them," Daddy had told her, squatting down at her side. "They're your sisters, and we love them. Everything will be fine."

Annika had groaned. "How can you tell her that in all good conscience? Because you can't possibly know. You've never been blind. Neither of us can be sure of what will become of them."

"They have us to protect them," her daddy had said with a nod. "That's all that children need."

"But what happens when we die? Who will they have then?" her mother had cried. "We have no family anywhere near."

"Me," Gretchen had said quietly as her fingers reached for

Trudy's dimpled elbow. "They'll have me. I won't let anything happen to them, Mommy. I promise."

And Gretchen had meant it.

The twins were eventually diagnosed as legally blind, their sight limited to discerning shadows and shapes, darkness and light. But there was nothing positive about their situation in Annika's eyes. When they went into town to visit the shops on Main Street, Annika would push Trudy and Bennie up the sidewalk in the double stroller and Gretchen would walk a few steps behind, peering into windows and listening to her mother bluntly answer those who asked, "How are your darling babies?"

"They are as blind as bats," she'd tell them, sounding as if it were the kiss of death. "I hope we can keep them with us and not be forced to send them to an institution."

Gretchen usually tried to remain silent and not challenge anything Annika said; but with each passing year, she had found it harder and harder not to chip in her two cents. "Bennie can hear the postman coming way before I can see him," she had finally dared to rebut, "and Trudy knows every spice in the rack by scent alone."

"Is that so?" Annika had said, her pale eyes narrowed.

"It is," Gretchen had replied, and had managed not to flinch, even though she knew it wasn't precisely the truth; merely a candy-coated lie. Bennie *could* hear things before anyone else, and Trudy *could* identify countless items by their smell alone.

Her sisters were special, Gretchen knew, regardless of what their mother believed, and she was determined to prove that they had no limitations.

So as the twins had grown, Gretchen had been their shepherd, watching over her sheep; taking them by the hand when they were old enough to walk, teaching them where every stick of furniture sat in the house, where every tree grew outside, where every step or gate or wall existed. Even more important, she reminded them over and over again that they were no less for not having eyeballs that worked like everyone else's.

"Maybe your gifts are in your other senses," she would tell them, and Bennie and Trudy would smile their precious smiles as if such a thing seemed perfectly reasonable.

When Gretchen was in the fifth grade, she learned that the school librarian, Miss Childs, had grown up with a blind mother and knew Braille well enough to instruct Bennie and Trudy. Miss Childs also took the liberty of ordering them Braille textbooks and such. Soon Gretchen's father asked the librarian outright if she'd become the girls' private tutor. She did such a good job with the twins that Annika ceased uttering the word "institution," and Gretchen's father seemed happier just having the very agreeable Miss Childs around.

By the time Gretchen was in high school, Bennie and Trudy had blossomed into capable young ladies, able to do all the things that Gretchen did around the house: dress themselves, tie bows in their hair, make their beds, clean their rooms, sweep the porch, and even climb the lowest branches of the maple tree out front. Thanks to Miss Childs, both girls were reading well beyond their grade levels. Indeed, Gretchen's father had become so fond of their tutor that he'd left to drive her home one day and had never returned.

I'm sorry, Anni—had read the note he'd left behind—*but I can't handle so much truth anymore. Sometimes ignorance is truly bliss, and what I need is more bliss in my life.*

Her mother had cried on Gretchen's shoulder, asking her, "Am I so horrible to be around? Am I that unlovable?"

Instead of being honest, Gretchen had told Annika what she knew her mother had wanted to hear, words cribbed from *Wanton Wild Love*, the romance novel she was in the midst of reading, tucked upstairs beneath her pillow. "Miss Childs was nothing but a temptress, Mother, a seductress out to lure away what belonged to another."

"Do you truly think so?"

"I do," she said, even though Miss Childs looked nothing like the half-naked woman with flowing red hair on the book's torrid cover. In her prim sweater sets and too long skirts, with her plain brown hair and bespectacled eyes, Miss Childs had appeared the very stereotype of what she was: a school librarian. Still, Gretchen's lie seemed to make Annika feel better so what was the harm?

It would not be the first nor the last time she fibbed to her mother.

In the year after her father left, during the summer before her senior year in high school, when Gretchen lost her virginity to a questionable young man and wound up pregnant, she lied to her mother again. Only that particular lie was different. That lie was a lot like her belly: it just kept growing and growing until it created a life all its own.

The Twister

And the stars of heaven fell unto the earth,
even as a fig tree casteth her untimely figs,
when she is shaken of a mighty wind.

BOOK OF REVELATIONS 6:13

Chapter One

April 2010

BAM BAM BAM!

Loose shutters banged against the house, pounding the clapboards like angry fists as the wind kicked up and howled around the eaves, drawing Gretchen Brink to the half-opened window above the kitchen sink.

A minute earlier, the sky had been a pristine blue, the April sun showering warmth upon the walnut farm while a gentle breeze ruffled the leaves of the just-bloomed peonies below the sill. Out of nowhere, fierce gusts forced their way through the window screen, batting at Gretchen's hair and stirring up the scent of rain and the rumble of thunder. Beyond her pale reflection in the glass, the sky turned black as pitch and a startling crack rent the air. A great *boom* followed as a bolt of lightning hit, causing her to see stars and jarring the floor beneath her feet.

"Good heavens," she said as goose bumps leaped across her flesh.

As quickly, the air turned an eerie shade that seemed a cross between gray and yellow. Some might call it green, but Gretchen could only describe it as menacing. Thunder crashed, rattling the glass. She jumped away as a downpour began to pelt the panes, blurring her line of sight; but not before she watched a gnarled branch ripped from a full-grown maple and hurled across the lawn as if made of feathers.

"Someone's angry," she said, rubbing the gooseflesh on her arms and wondering what had nature so riled up that it wrested branches from trees and tossed about everything that wasn't fastened down.

"Gretchen! We must get to the cellar this instant," the elder of her twin sisters, Bennie, declared as she came up from behind; hands outstretched as she felt her way into the room, the creaking floor announcing her every step. Bennie stopped before a high-backed chair and tightly grasped it, tilting her head ceiling-ward though her milky eyes stayed downcast. "Can't you hear it?" Her round face grew grim. "It's close, and it's coming straight at us."

"What's coming toward us? I can't hear anything above the wind," Gretchen said, and tensed just the same, because what *she* could hear didn't matter. Bennie might have been blind since birth but she had ears like a bat. She could sense impending disaster more accurately than a meteorologist's Doppler radar.

"A twister," Bennie said quite plainly, and her chin began to quiver. "It's dropped right out of the sky very near, and it's on its way. We're dead in its path."

"Where's Trudy?" Gretchen asked, trying hard not to panic.

She knew good and well that tornadoes didn't mess around, not when they plowed through tiny Missouri towns, and Walnut Ridge was about as tiny as they came. A twister's only job was to make a mess of all it touched. They had been lucky these thirty-nine years since her Abby was born, the bumpiest weather seeming to miraculously bypass the farm; but maybe their luck had run out.

"Trudy!" Gretchen began to shout, heading for the dining room as the thunder and shrieking winds shook the house. "Trude, where are you?"

"I'm here," the younger twin called back, appearing beneath the curve of the arch separating dining room from kitchen.

Trudy looked the mirror image of Bennie: round head fringed with faded brown stuck atop a thin neck and slight frame, with slender arms and legs far stronger than they appeared. She was forever clad in cotton smocks with ample pockets to carry odds and ends, like tissues, bits of string, and treats for her cat, Matilda. In fact, at that very moment, she clutched Matilda to her breasts, not about to let her go, despite how the hairless feline wiggled and squirmed.

"It's bad, isn't it?" Trudy said, scurrying toward Gretchen as another boom of thunder shook the tiny farmhouse. "I can smell the change in the air. It reeks of anguish and unfinished business."

"Bennie says a twister's headed straight for us, and she's never been wrong."

"No, she's never wrong," Trudy grimly agreed.

And Trudy's nose had never been wrong, either.

Matilda mewed, her pale skin stretching over her skeletal body as she climbed toward Trudy's shoulder. Gretchen took her sister's arm and hurried her through the kitchen and to the stairs, descending behind Bennie, whose heavy clogs clip-clopped down the steps.

"It's so dad-gummed dusty, like I'm breathing in the musty scent of every soul who's ever lived here," Trudy remarked, and sneezed, losing a startled Matilda from her shoulder in the process. The tiny feet padded lickety-split into the cellar and out of sight.

"It's a hundred-year-old basement, Trude," Bennie said, her voice made hollow by the stone walls surrounding them. "It's practically made of dust."

At the top of the stairs, Gretchen shut and latched the door for good measure before she trailed the twins below-ground, to where the dirt floors and rock walls were lit only by a single sixty-watt bulb. She found the flashlight she kept at the base of the steps, switching it on just as the electricity flickered and went out.

Though she paused in the darkness as she swung the beam of the flashlight to guide her, her sisters didn't hesitate in the least. They had no need for light to lead them. They knew every inch of the old house tactilely. They hadn't grown up inside its walls, but they'd been living within them for nearly as long as Gretchen. She'd moved them in with her four decades ago when she was barely eighteen and they were just thirteen, once she'd inherited the place from Lily and Cooper Winston, a year after she'd given birth to Abby. "Sam would want his daughter to grow up here, nowhere else," Lily had insisted, and Gretchen had not disagreed. Just as the home had been a cozy nest for Sam Winston and two generations of his family before him, it had quickly become Abby's and Gretchen's home-sweet-home as well.

Dear Sam, God rest his soul.

The place still rightly belonged to him, as far as Gretchen was concerned; but she'd stopped feeling guilty for being there. She loved it as deeply as anyone could, and every inch of it was a constant reminder of him and how his selflessness had saved her.

She told herself that caring for the farm as much as she did was repayment enough for her betrayal, even if she wasn't entirely convinced.

"It's at the fence line already," Bennie said, interrupting Gretchen's thoughts.

"And it's getting closer."

The three of them settled into a tiny room with rounded walls where a trio of metal folding chairs awaited them.

Bennie reached for Trudy's hand and clutched it. "Oh my, it's barreling up the front drive. Can you feel it shake the ground?"

"Oh my, oh my, oh my," Trudy echoed.

Gretchen didn't feel the ground move so much as she felt

Matilda padding back and forth between her ankles. The noise of the wind was less fierce below-ground and still she heard a high-pitched keening, angry and insistent.

As she settled into the tight circle with her sisters, a large pop rent the air and then a crash that made the small house shudder. Gretchen dropped the flashlight from her hands, and it clattered somewhere near her feet.

Matilda hissed as if telling her, *Watch where you put that thing!*

"Please, Lord, protect us," Trudy whispered, and Gretchen reached for her sisters' hands, grabbing on when she connected; all of them trembling.

Please don't let us die down here, and I swear I'll never tell another lie, Gretchen squeezed her eyes closed and prayed, though she didn't entirely mean it.

Chapter Two

"It's not possible. It can't be."

Despite what appeared to be the cold, hard facts, Abigail Brink simply refused to believe that she was pregnant.

Even the queasiness that gripped her sporadically from dawn to dusk, the bloated belly, the pressing need to frequently relieve herself, and the two missed periods weren't enough to completely convince her. These were all things caused by stress and she certainly had that in spades. The small art gallery in Chicago's Lincoln Park where she'd directed sales for the past eight years had been gradually cutting back on staff and was forever on the precipice of closing, thanks to newly budget-conscious customers and shrinking commissions. She couldn't afford to lose her job, not when she would have to pay the rent solo since Nate had moved out.

Abby felt quite a lot like a walking cliché: on the precipice of forty, careening toward a mid-life crisis, and barely holding it together. So she couldn't be pregnant, not now of all times. Having a baby didn't fit into her plans, and it made no sense besides.

"It just can't be," she kept telling herself, because she'd heard statistics on women her age conceiving naturally and the numbers bordered on anemic. Still, somewhere in the back of her head there was a tiny seed of hope it might be true.

To stop herself from second-guessing, she went by the drugstore on her way home from work, buying a new toothbrush, a bar of soap, and a box of First Response. Not even bothering to take off her coat, she'd shut herself into the bathroom and locked the door despite being the only one there. Since their argument weeks before, Nate had moved across town and was camping out on the couch of his brother, Myron.

Gulping down water in between, she somehow managed to pee on all three plastic sticks by the end of an hour, and she stared at each for a full ten minutes until every blank oval had sported twin pink lines.

Pregnant. Pregnant. Pregnant.

Though the package insert illustrated that she was clearly knocked up, a tiny warning indicated that women aged forty and up might show false positives because of something called pituitary HCG. Abby had months to go before she gave up thirty-nine for good, but it was enough to fan the seeds of doubt.

She showed up bright and early at her doctor's office the

following morning, waiting to have blood drawn, all the while trying to convince herself that she had something else, like mono, Epstein-Barr, or anemia. Surely those things could throw over-the-counter pregnancy results off-kilter, and any one of those diagnoses made more sense, considering how she'd been regularly missing meals and rest.

And still, she couldn't concentrate on work or sleep that night, pondering what the blood tests would reveal. She stayed awake, gazing at the ceiling, wondering how this could be happening to her at such an inopportune time.

When Dr. Epps had phoned the next afternoon with her lab results, Abby couldn't help but ask, "What's the verdict?" all the while gnawing on a coarse bit of skin near her thumbnail. "Please tell me all I need are iron pills or a vacation."

"Well, I'd hardly advise any patient against a vacation, but that won't change the facts. Everything's perfectly normal but . . ." There, Dr. Epps had hesitated.

"But what?" Abby had asked, biting the inside of her cheek and tasting blood.

"Congratulations, Abigail. You're absolutely, one hundred percent pregnant."

"You're sure?"

"Sure as shootin'," the doctor had chirped. "We should set up an ultrasound so we can figure out better how far along you are, although your hormone level's consistent with seven or eight weeks. We also need to get you on prenatal vitamins. Should I turn you over to Nancy to make the appointment?"

"Um, no, not just yet," Abby had mumbled, "I'll have to call back, okay?"

At which point she'd dropped the phone to the floor and stood with her mouth open, eyes wide, and knees wobbling, certain she was having an anxiety attack. When she'd recovered enough to cross the kitchen, she'd grabbed the calendar from the refrigerator door, counting backward, trying to figure things out.

Had she and Nathan even had sex those two months past? They'd been growing increasingly distant since New Year's, and it was both of their faults. Though, really, all it took was once, right? One night without a condom when a single sperm got lucky enough to do the deed. If only they hadn't argued, she thought; if only they hadn't been living such separate lives. How Abby wished things were different, how desperately she wanted to call Nate straightaway and say, *Babe! You're not going to believe this!* But she couldn't.

She had to quit staring at the calendar when her eyes began to blur. She was too tired to pinpoint dates, exhausted by long days at the gallery and late evenings squirreled away in the spare bedroom with her easel and paints, deliberately avoiding the things that were missing from their relationship. And if she'd been hiding out, Nate had been no better, burying himself in his laptop, endlessly working on new apps and often disappearing at odd hours for meetings at coffeehouses, clearly more committed to his goals than to Abby.

Her last attempt to put them on the right path had failed miserably. "We need to do something about our situation," she had confronted him two weeks before after gathering up the courage to instigate the kind of conversation she knew Nate dreaded most. "We can't go on this way. It's not healthy."

"If it ain't broke," he had countered. And though he'd grinned a nervous grin, Abby had read the panic in his eyes.

Any stabs at discussing their living arrangements always made Nathan so jumpy. She could mention something as simple as needing new silverware, and he took it as a prelude to a lengthy discourse on the M word. Maybe it was her small-town roots or being raised without her father, but Abby had a traditional streak that went beyond the need to share a bed and an apartment. She'd always assumed that living together would eventually lead to marriage; but as she found herself wanting to nest more and more, she'd sadly realized that Nate wasn't quite so willing and able.

"I feel like I'm floundering," she'd told him, and not for the first time. "Don't you want to move forward instead of running in place?" she'd asked. "Don't you want to make this permanent before it's too late?"

"When is it too late? There's nothing wrong with taking the proper time to figure things out," he had replied as if reminding her that six years together didn't ensure that they were meant to be. "My parents were married twenty years before they divorced," he'd added, his routine argument in such a case. "There are never guarantees that how you're feeling today will be precisely what you're feeling tomorrow."

Okay, sure, Abby understood that his folks' splitting up had traumatized him, but she'd never known how much until she'd experienced his resistance to lifelong commitment. Unless it was just a convenient excuse for him. Either way, his argument was getting old, as was she. If you truly loved someone, she believed, being with them forever should feel right; destined even.

"There aren't guarantees for anything," she'd remarked, another tidbit she'd thrown at him over and over. "My mom didn't even have a chance to marry my dad before he went overseas, and I know she always regretted not asking him to stay."

Gretchen Brink had never married, had never even been in love with anyone else but Sam Winston, so far as Abby was aware. Not that her mother had said as much outright, but it was clear in the way she behaved, in her tone of voice and the softening of her eyes whenever she mentioned Sam's name. Abby didn't want to end up like that, alone and always wondering what could have been. She and Nate had to seize the day. No one could see into the future. They could both live another fifty years or fall off the el platform onto the tracks and get run over tomorrow.

Because, when it came down to it, Abby truly loved Nathan March. If Nate's passion was equally intense, then expressing his commitment to her—say, in the form of an engagement—seemed perfectly reasonable.

"Love is all you need," she had insisted because she believed it.

Nate had merely sniffed. "That's a Beatles song, not reality."

But Abigail had always believed that songs, like art, often revealed universal truths, and the fact that love made the world go round was one of them. What she wanted was an unshakable commitment to a future together, not a roommate who paid for pizza and kissed her and told her she was sexy (however nice all of those things might be). It took everything she had to finally put her foot down and give him an ultimatum.

"If you're not sure in this moment that you want to be with me forever, then I think you should move out until you make up your mind."

"You want me to go?" At first, Nate had seemed truly stunned. Then he'd burst out laughing. "You're joking right? You're kicking me to the curb because I don't share your fairy-tale view of marriage?"

"I'm not kicking you anywhere, Nathan. I'm merely suggesting that you leave until you decide whether I'm The One or not," Abby had explained in the clearest way possible.

He had arched a furry eyebrow. "*The One?* Do you know how archaic that sounds?"

"Maybe to you, but not to me." The more he seemed to mock her, the angrier she'd become. How could he be so dense, as if after six years together he had no clue about her desires? It was as though when it came to marriage, he had a complete mental block. "If you don't know for certain and you think there's someone better for you out there, I can't have you around. I turn forty this year. I don't have time to waste, and I need to know I'm as important to you as you are to me. Right now, I have my doubts."

"C'mon, Abs, this isn't funny." He had stared at her until his smile died, finally grasping the idea that she wasn't joking around. "You're really serious?"

"Totally."

"Wow." His Adam's apple had bobbed, his wide forehead pleating. "You know I love you or I wouldn't be here. I would have left ages ago. But I stay because I wake up in the morning and want to be with you that day. Isn't that enough?" Heat had flushed his cheeks. "Do you want me to drop down on bended knee and propose? Should I promise you forever because it's what you want to hear?"

"No"—she had shaken her head as tears stung her eyes—"not if you don't really mean it."

He'd pinched his lips together, looking pained, and his hazel eyes had darkened, wounded. "I'll do whatever you want," he finally told her, grudgingly. "It's your call, and maybe you're right. Maybe we both need some space to think."

"Yes, space to think," she'd agreed, though it tore her in two just to say it.

And, just like that, Nate had stuffed his gym bag with underwear, T-shirts, socks, toothbrush, and toothpaste. He had held her hand for a moment before he'd walked out the door, mumbling something about crashing with Myron until she came to her senses. His head low, he'd dragged his heels down the hallway as though, any minute, she would call him back and tell him she didn't mean it; that having a ring on her finger didn't matter.

But it did. It really did.

So Abby had shut and bolted the door behind him, thinking that any minute she would hear his key in the lock; that he'd come back and blubber that she was most assuredly The One and he couldn't live without her.

Five minutes passed, then twenty more, until an hour had gone by and Abigail had ascertained that he wasn't returning. At least not right away. She had messed up her bed and now she had to lie in it.

That fight seemed so long ago, especially since her call from Dr. Epps. Two weeks apart from Nate felt like years; fourteen long days in which they had spoken only a few times when he'd phoned to say he needed to drop by to pick up a gadget or more underwear. Abby had been careful not to be anywhere around when he did. That would have only confused her all the more.

Despite how she considered herself an independent woman, she felt unsettled and weak without him, as if she'd removed an internal organ required to properly function. Then to hear that she was having a baby. Nate's baby.

It was almost too much to take.

Abby knew she couldn't stay in the apartment alone, not while she was so aware of the new life taking root inside her; the tiny seed of a baby that was partly Nate's, too. If she was going to get through this, if she was going to figure things out, it wouldn't be here. She couldn't tell Nate. She refused to have him beholden to her because of her pregnancy. If he came back—if they decided to make a go of it again—it had to be because of love and love alone.

She couldn't explain to her friends in Chicago, because they were Nate's friends, too. They would spill the beans to him, and she wasn't ready for that yet.

The only place where she could take refuge was home. She craved a chance to pause and draw in a deep breath. Lots of deep breaths. Becoming a mother changed everything, and she was sure her own mom would understand better than most. When Gretchen had given birth to Abby, she had done it alone, and Abby needed reminding that such a fate wasn't the end of the world.

Besides, she felt inexplicably drawn to the farmhouse where she'd been raised. She yearned to soak in its calm and sleep in her old bed in the room that had once been her father's—the father she'd thought about so often as a child, the one she'd wished so hard would return every time she'd blown out a candle on a birthday cake. Though she'd never met the man, he still loomed large in her life. Samuel Henry Winston, son of a walnut farmer, grandson of a rainmaker, and "the best friend I ever had," according to her mother.

Abby had only his photograph, one Gretchen had given her ages ago, of a teenager in overalls with a long face, dark hair, and piercing eyes. "He was like no one else, attuned to nature in ways most folks aren't," her mom had said. "When Sam wept, the clouds would open wide and cry with him," Gretchen would explain while Abby ate up every word like a favorite bedtime story. "And when he smiled one of his rare smiles, the sun beamed so brightly it was blinding."

"Do you figure he can see me?" Abby would frequently ask, and her mother had replied with an ebullient nod. "I have a feeling he's watching you always and that he's much nearer than you think. If he could find his way back, he would, I'm sure of it."

Just as Abby needed to find her way back now.

Perhaps the baby was a sign that she'd gotten off track,

that she'd lived her life according to Nate for so long that she'd pushed aside what was most important. Her mom and her aunts. The farm. The family. Her dad.

"We're going home," she said, and put a hand on her belly. Exhaling softly, she picked up her cell phone, hesitating but a second before she dialed Walnut Ridge. Her mother's phone rang and rang and rang without an answer, which was concerning. Someone was always around the house, if not Gretchen then Aunt Bennie or Aunt Trudy.

She hung up and tried again only to get a rapid busy signal.

Maybe they were having trouble with the lines. Could be a squirrel had chewed through them again. That had happened on more than one occasion, and it took the devil to get the service truck out to the old farm for repairs.

Well, no matter, she told herself, ending the call. She'd call the office and tell Alan she was taking some sick days. Then she'd pack a bag and catch a cab to the train station. Her mom had told her over and over again, "If ever you need me, I'm here for you, any day, rain or shine."

And, at the moment, Abby needed her something fierce.

About the Author

Susan McBride is the author of women's fiction, including *The Truth About Love and Lightning*, *Little Black Dress*, and *The Cougar Club*, as well as the award-winning Debutante Dropout Mysteries. She calls herself an "accidental cougar" after meeting a man nine years younger in 2005 when she was a *St. Louis Magazine* "top single." They were married in February 2008 and live happily ever after in a suburb of St. Louis. She is nearing her six-year mark as a breast cancer survivor and often speaks to women's groups about her experience. In January 2012, she was named one of St. Louis's "Most Dynamic People of the Year" by the *Ladue News*. In April 2012, she was given the "Survivor of the Year" Award by the St. Louis affiliate of Susan G. Komen for the Cure. On June 28, 2012, she and her husband had their first child, Emily, who weighed in at a robust eight pounds. As Susan likes to say, "Life is never boring."